JanBraai
THE VEGETARIAN OPTION

This book is dedicated to the millions of South Africans who celebrate National Braai Day on 24 September every year.

In National Braai Day, we South Africans have a realistic opportunity to entrench and cement a national day of celebration for our country, within our lifetimes. I believe that having a national day of celebration can play a significant role in nation-building and social cohesion as the observance of our shared heritage can truly bind us together.

In Africa, a fire is the traditional place of gathering. I urge you to get together with your friends and family around a fire on 24 September every year to celebrate our heritage, share stories and pass on traditions. Please help me spread that word!

CONTENTS

INTRODUCTION

I am not a vegetarian, but I prepare and eat many dishes that can be classified as vegetarian, and vegetarians have always been very welcome at my braai fire. In fact, what I consider to be arguably the single most popular braai meal in South Africa is a vegetarian one – the braaibroodjie (see page 14).

Since the inception of the National Braai Day initiative in 2005, we've been quite clear about our goal, which is to establish and position 24 September as South Africa's national day of celebration. On this day, the collective 'we' encourage all citizens to connect around a fire, share our heritage and wave our flag. Quite logically, many of the citizens of our great nation who I wish to see united around fires on National Braai Day every year, are individuals who, by choice or for whatever other reason, do not eat meat. For me, it's very simple: if the food is cooked on a fire, it's a braai – no matter what that food might be. And so it gives me immense pleasure to be able to publish a book filled with fantastic braai recipes that all happen not to include meat.

Some recipes in this book were taken as is from my prior books, as I have obviously published vegetarian recipes in the past – this is just a book where all recipes fit that criteria. The balance of the recipes are some of my old favourites, adjusted to replace the meat with an ingredient or ingredients that will give you the same flavour profile. And then there are also new recipes, developed from scratch. Once you set your recipe-development parameters to 'anything goes, as long as there's no meat', the creative process around the braai fire leads you to wonderful places.

The publication of this book might seem like a natural progression from my previous books, but a material chunk of credit for what you're holding in your hands

right now must still go to Brad and Candice Gale. I know Brad from my school days when, although we were from different sides of Cape Town's boerewors curtain, we competed against each other in triathlons. We lost touch but reconnected over social media in recent years, and while Brad now spends more time in the swimming pool and I prefer to cycle, we still occasionally chat online.

About a year before the publication of this book, Brad sent me a message, which by his own admission, was a shot in the dark. His problem, he said, was that he loves to braai and often does so using my books but his wife is a vegetarian. He asked if I would ever consider publishing a purely vegetarian book. And I have to admit, once I started to consider how much sense this made, I was almost embarrassed that I hadn't already published such a book. I could think of absolutely no legitimate reason why there is no Jan Braai recipe book for vegetarians like Candice.

And so, to every single braai-loving South African who simply chooses not to eat meat, I am sorry that it took me so long. Here is your book. I hope you enjoy it.

Thank you to every person who, over the years, has shared braai tips, advice and secrets with me. The treasure chest of tacit knowledge I have comes from many conversations and shared meals with other people who like to braai. I am thankful, honoured and privileged to have the opportunity to share and spread some of this knowledge through my books.

Finally, thank you to the close family, real friends and loyal colleagues who surround me. These are the people who support me in my job and everyday life – and most importantly, who braai with me most often.

Jan Braai

MEASUREMENTS IN *THE VEGETARIAN OPTION*

I hope that anyone reading this book will already have purchased and read at least one of my previous books. But if this is your first JanBraai experience, then here are some basic guidelines for measuring ingredients at the fire.

A TEASPOON IS 5 ML

A teaspoon is what you stir your tea with. At kitchen and homeware shops or in the kitchenware area of a supermarket, you can buy measuring teaspoons that are exactly 5 ml big when you fill them flat (not heaped). If you do not have a real measuring teaspoon that is exactly 5 ml, just use a heaped amount on a normal sized tea-stirring teaspoon as it will be close enough. In the recipes, I have abbreviated teaspoon to tsp.

A TOT IS 25 ML

A tot is that little glass that you drink shots from in a bar. In South Africa, the legal size of one measurement of such types of alcohol is 25 ml. These little glasses are widely available across the country in both glass and plastic forms. Over the years, I've generally found that the worse a kitchen is equipped, the better the chances that you will find tot glasses somewhere in the house. A student's house or bachelor's flat are prime examples.

A CUP IS 250 ML

The sharp braaier will know that 250 ml is also a quarter of a litre, which is 1 000 ml. To make it simple, many liquid food ingredients are sold by the cup, most noticeably, cream. If you do not have a measuring cup available, first look if one of the ingredients in the recipe you are making came in a 250 ml container, and use that. Otherwise, a normal tea cup will be close enough.

HALF A CUP IS 125 ML

No surprises here! But you will be amazed at the questions some people ask me on the JanBraai Facebook page while I'm lighting the fire before watching some rugby on a Saturday afternoon. When out and about, you can just judge half a cup with the eye but in the long run, it's worth buying one of these measurement tools. Kitchenware shops and kitchen departments in supermarkets sell them. It says ½ cup on the device and when you fill it flat, it contains 125 ml.

9

BRAAI-
BROODJIES
& BURGERS

TRADITIONAL BRAAIBROODJIE

This is the original South African braaibroodjie recipe. It's how my parents taught me and how their parents taught them. I love braaibroodjies exactly like this and millions of other people have too. I also regularly braai many other types of braaibroodjies. I research, experiment, and push the boundaries. The recipes for some of my other favourites and most popular braaibroodjies are also in this book. But this is the original recipe for a braaibroodjie and you do it exactly as described here. Any deviation is exactly that – a deviation from the original.

WHAT YOU NEED
(makes 10 braaibroodjies)

butter

1 sliced white bread loaf (with at least 20 slices)

chutney

400 g Cheddar cheese (sliced or grated)

4 tomatoes (sliced – you need 2 slices per braaibroodjie and there are, on average, 5 useable slices per tomato)

1 large onion (sliced into rings)

salt and pepper

WHAT TO DO TO ASSEMBLE

1. Butter one side of all bread slices.
2. Place half the bread slices buttered side down; spread chutney on them and evenly distribute all the cheese, tomato and onion on top. Grind salt and pepper over that.
3. Cover with the remaining bread slices, buttered side facing up. Some people try and make an issue out of whether to butter the braaibroodjie on the outside or inside. There is no debate: you butter it on the outside. This makes a golden-brown finished product, and also keeps the braaibroodjie from sticking to the grid.

WHAT TO DO TO BRAAI

Braaibroodjies are always braaied in a toeklaprooster (hinged grid). Using an open grid for this is silly to the point of stupid. You want very gentle heat and you need to turn them often. They are ready when the outsides are golden brown, the cheese has melted and all the other ingredients are properly heated all the way through. If the outsides are burnt before the cheese is melted, you've failed.

AND ...

If you're having a breakfast braai then fry a few eggs sunny side up in a pan on the braai or stove, and when your braaibroodjies are finished, gently pull them open and insert one egg into each. You now have a breakfast braaibroodjie.

MUSHROOM BURGERS

This is a revolutionary burger. It's the vegetarian burger that non-vegetarians love. I like to make them using those normal supermarket burger rolls with no substance, as it keeps the focus on the mushroom.

WHAT YOU NEED
(feeds 6)

6 soft burger rolls
plain cream cheese
6 giant mushrooms
garlic butter
feta cheese (I like the kind with bits of black pepper but any type will do)

WHAT TO DO

1. Slice the rolls and spread cream cheese onto the bottom half of each roll.
2. Braai the mushrooms on medium-to-hot coals until nicely browned and fairly soft, for a total of about 6–8 minutes. Braai them for 3 minutes with the bottom (black) side facing downwards. Then flip them over, scoop a bit of garlic butter into each and then braai with the top (white) side facing downwards until they are soft. They turn quite easily and if you are gentle they will not break apart, so either an open or hinged grid is fine.
3. Put one mushroom on each prepared roll and crumble feta cheese over that.
4. The burgers can be eaten immediately and juices from the mushrooms will seep into the roll as you eat.

WHAT TO DO FOR GARLIC BUTTER
Very simply you mix chopped garlic and butter. If you have parsley on hand you chop that and mix it in as well. For 6 mushrooms you'll need 1–2 tots of butter, 1–2 cloves of garlic and ½ tot of parsley.

CAPE-STYLE BRAAIBROODJIE

One Saturday afternoon, ahead of a Saturday night braai, Natasha, who sent me this recipe, designed this take on a braaibroodjie. According to her, the inspiration was the Cape Town habit of serving preserved green figs with everything. Truth be told, I am from Cape Town; I love preserved green figs, and I think this recipe is absolutely brilliant, so well done to Natasha!

WHAT YOU NEED
(feeds 8)

2 red onions (sliced into rings)

olive oil or butter

16 slices white bread

soft butter (to spread over the slices)

300 g mozzarella cheese (grated)

1 small tub (200 g) **black pepper-flavoured feta cheese** (crumbled)

8 preserved green figs (chopped into small chunks)

WHAT TO DO

1. Caramelise or brown the sliced onions with a bit of oil or butter in a pan or pot on the fire or stove.
2. Butter all 16 slices of bread on one side and lay 8 of the slices, buttered side down, onto a large tray.
3. Evenly distribute the caramelised onions, grated mozzarella, crumbled feta and chopped figs between the 8 laid-out slices of bread and then close with the remaining 8 slices, buttered side facing outwards and upwards.
4. Put the prepared braaibroodjies into a hinged grid and braai over medium-hot coals, turning very regularly, until they're golden brown on the outside and the cheese has melted on the inside.

AND ...

There is no and. This is perfect as is.

GREEK-STYLE BRAAIBROODJIE

Two of the most popular side dishes to the South African braai are the traditional braaibroodjie and a Greek salad. They usually meet on the plate. But then I decided to rather let some of the ingredients meet a bit earlier. It was a very successful meeting.

To make it work, you sauté the onion and green pepper in a bit of olive oil beforehand. This sweetens them and serves the dual purpose of making it easier to actually fit everything into the braaibroodjies. Olives, feta, tomatoes and Cheddar cheese complete the picture. These braaibroodjies are quite bulky and need to be braaied with care. Best practice is to use a hinged grid of adjustable width.

WHAT YOU NEED
(feeds 4)

1 tot olive oil (and more to drizzle over the bread)

1 green bell pepper (sliced)

1 red onion (sliced)

8 slices white bread

½ cup olives (halved and pitted)

2 wheels feta cheese (about 150 g, crumbled)

1 cup Cheddar cheese (grated)

2 big red tomatoes (sliced)

salt and pepper

1 tot fresh oregano

WHAT TO DO

1. Heat the oil in a pan and sauté the pepper and onion until soft and caramelised. This will take about 15 minutes, so be patient.
2. Drizzle all the bread slices with olive oil on one side (these oiled sides will be the outsides).
3. Put half of the slices of bread, oiled side down, on a plate and layer with the olives, sautéed onion and green pepper, feta cheese, Cheddar cheese and tomato slices. Season with salt, pepper and oregano.
4. Close with the other bread slices, oiled side to the outside, and braai in a hinged grid over a medium heat until the bread is toasted and the cheese melted.

AND ...

Although an ingredient of Greek salad, cucumbers are not welcome in these braaibroodjies. Rather serve it as garnish on the side. A real Greek salad never contains lettuce so you don't need lettuce in either the braaibroodjies or on the side. Apart from the cucumber then, these braaibroodjies contain all the ingredients of a braaibroodjie and a Greek salad. It's delicious, completely multipurpose and cuts out those annoying untouched bowls of salad at the braai.

THE ICED TEA SANDWICH

The British on their muddy island off the west coast of Europe do a soft version of this sandwich and serve it with tea. But here in Africa we know how to make fires and we know how to braai.

WHAT YOU NEED
(feeds 4)

4 big baby marrows (big enough that the slices will not fall through your grid)

good-quality olive oil

freshly ground salt and pepper

1 lemon (juice)

8 slices normal white bread (the completely normal sliced white bread)

butter (to spread on the outside of the bread slices)

½ cup full-fat plain cream cheese

TO SERVE
rooibos tea

fruit juice of your choice

ice

a few lemons

WHAT TO DO

1. Use a vegetable peeler to peel the baby marrows into nice thin strips. If you have a well-equipped kitchen and own a mandolin, use that. Once you have peeled all the marrows, place them in a bowl and drizzle with olive oil, then add salt and pepper, and squeeze the lemon juice over them.
2. Now pack the seasoned baby marrow ribbons on your grid and braai over medium coals until they are showing a few char marks. Carefully turn them around. I say 'carefully' as due to their size and texture, they have a tendency to escape the grid and kamikaze it straight into the coals. You definitely only need to turn once and as soon as they have personality, you can take them off.
3. Now assemble the braaibroodjies. Butter all the bread slices on one side, which will be the outside. Divide and spread the cream cheese onto the non-buttered sides of half of the slices. Top with braaied baby marrow ribbons, then close the braaibroodjies with the leftover slices of bread, buttered sides facing upwards.
4. Place into your hinged grid and braai over medium heat, turning once or thrice until the outsides are golden brown and toasted. Cut into triangles and serve immediately.

AND …

The traditional way is to serve these with iced tea. You prepare that by combining half and half measures of cooled rooibos tea with the fruit juice of your choice and serving that over ice with a slice and squeeze of fresh lemon.

ITALIAN BRAAI BRUSCHETTA

Italy is a very pleasant place to visit, and I also like their food. The climate is agreeable and similar to South Africa, and many of the ingredients I like to braai with in South Africa are also widely available there. Their flag is beautiful – almost as photogenic as our own South African flag – and there are some famous Italian meals mimicking the colours of their flag, the Caprese salad of tomato, sweet basil and buffalo mozzarella probably being the best known. This braai snack, firmly based on the original Italian version, has the same famous tricolour scheme and more. But the real difference is that we're braaing tomatoes and adding some fire-toast flavour to the bread as well to end up with bruschetta that I honestly think is better than the original Italian.

WHAT YOU NEED
(feeds 6–8 as a snack)

1 French baguette (sliced)
200 g feta cheese (crumbled)

FOR THE OLIVE OIL SPREAD
4 garlic cloves (crushed and chopped)
few sprigs of fresh thyme
1 tsp salt
2 tots olive oil

FOR THE TOMATO SALAD
500 g cherry tomatoes
(roughly chopped)
1 tot olive oil
1 tot balsamic vinegar
salt and pepper (to taste)
bunch of fresh basil
(roughly chopped)

FOR THE TOMATO SKEWERS
500 g cherry, Mediterranean cocktail or Roma tomatoes
(the idea is that they should skewer whole onto the skewer)
skewers

WHAT TO DO

1. Make the olive oil spread. Place the garlic, thyme and salt into your mortar, and use the pestle to make a smooth paste. Add the olive oil and mix well. If you don't have a pestle and mortar, chop everything together as finely as possible and add the olive oil. Now lather all of the bread slices with the olive oil spread on one side.
2. Make the tomato salad by mixing the tomatoes, olive oil and balsamic vinegar in a bowl. Add salt, pepper and basil to taste.
3. Place the whole tomatoes on the skewers and braai over hot coals until roasted and charred. They should just start to burst and crack a little bit.
4. Lightly toast the bread slices on a grid over medium-hot coals with the oiled side facing down.
5. Build your braaied bruschetta by starting with the toasted bread, oiled side up, topping with tomato salad, then feta cheese and ending with the roasted tomatoes from the skewers.

AND ...

Use different coloured and types of tomatoes for the skewers to add a bit of variety to the bruschetta.

THREE-CHEESE BRAAIBROODJIE

The South African braaibroodjie has evolved, taking on a life of its own. The original recipe will always be a crowd-pleaser and world-cup winner, but the new democratic South Africa found that there are many other fantastic ways to make braaibroodjies. This one is a celebration of the basic braaibroodjie's core ingredient – cheese. The wider the variety of cheese, the better. For this recipe, I like to go with three types that are widely available but if you have other types on hand in your fridge, by all means use those. Experiment and make this recipe your own!

WHAT YOU NEED
(feeds 10)

20 slices white bread

butter (to spread over the slices)

1 tot Dijon mustard

1 tot wholegrain mustard

3 tots mayonnaise

240 g Cheddar cheese
(I prefer mature)

240 g Gouda (I prefer mature)

100 g blue cheese

WHAT TO DO

1. Butter each slice of bread on one side (the buttered sides will be on the outside of the braaibroodjies).
2. Now lay out 10 slices of bread with the buttered side down and spread with Dijon mustard, wholegrain mustard and mayonnaise.
3. Next, grate, slice or crumble the cheese, and evenly distribute it onto the slices of the mustard-coated bread.
4. Put the other 10 bread slices on top, buttered side facing upwards.
5. Place the prepared sandwiches in a hinged grid and close the grid. This makes braaing easier and will also help to compress the bread into a correct braaibroodjie shape.
6. Braai over medium-hot coals, turning often, until the outside of the bread is golden brown and the cheese is melted all the way through.

AND ...

This recipe was originally designed to be served with a glass of cold white wine, but that is really up to you.

CAMEMBERT BURGER

Compared to some of my other favourite cheeses, Camembert has a fairly low melting point. The outside skin has a much higher melting point than the inside though, which makes it the perfect cheese to braai as is. For the braaing part, there is no need to put it in bread, in a pan or in foil: just take it out of the packaging and braai the cheese over medium to low coals for about 10 minutes until the cheese on the inside has melted, but before the outside skin melts, boils or ruptures.

You need fairly insubstantial burger rolls for this one, of a personality that will not overshadow the cheese. The basic supermarket burger roll works well but if you're popping into the artisan bakery, aim for a more cocktail-sized sourdough roll, rather than the mango-sized giant roll that no mortal person can actually fit into their mouth.

WHAT YOU NEED
(feeds 4)

1 tot olive oil

2 red onions (sliced)

½ tot balsamic vinegar

2 whole rounds Camembert cheese (about 125 g each)

4 soft burger rolls

butter or olive oil

fig jam

rocket

WHAT TO DO

1. Heat oil in your fireproof pan and fry the onions over hot flames until soft and caramelised. This is the first step as you can perform it while the fire is still burning and you're waiting for the coals to be ready. When you like the look of the onions, add a dash of balsamic vinegar to the pan, let that cook off and now set the pan and its contents aside.

2. Braai the Camembert cheese rounds on an open grid (I don't like the pressure a closed hinged grid puts on them). You don't want the coals to be too hot as you want the insides to melt before the outsides burn or break. Turn them about three times during the braai, using either your recently washed hands or a clean pair of braai tongs. If you're using tongs to turn them, take care not to press too hard and damage the cheese. You will be able to feel when the cheese is ready (when it goes soft on the inside) and it absolutely is ready when some part of the rind ruptures or pops open and cheese starts to ooze out.

3. Cut each burger roll in half and butter the insides or drizzle with olive oil. During the last minute or two of the braai, also toast the insides of your burger buns on the grid until golden brown.

4. Lather the toasted insides of all the burger rolls with fig jam.

5. Assemble the burger by placing the rocket leaves at the bottom.

6. Slice each braaied Camembert in half and add that to the tower of awesome, followed by caramelised onions.

7. Close each roll and serve immediately while the cheese is still soft and melted.

CHOCOLATE BRAAIBROODJIE

Many people are of the opinion that a braaibroodjie is the best meal in the world and it's a view I often share. My love for this meal is clear from the number of braaibroodjie recipes in this book. For those who understand me or follow my career, especially via the television show, it makes sense that at some stage I would arrive at a dessert braaibroodjie. Now you can have braaibroodjies for starters, main meals and dessert.

I designed this recipe to conclude an episode of *Jan Braai vir Erfenis* during the 2018 season, and there was a countrywide shortage of chocolate spread in the week after the episode aired. As one father put it to me on the Jan Braai Facebook page: 'We drove to a supermarket that Friday night right after the episode aired and as we walked into the supermarket, another father with his kids passed us on their way out of the door with white bread and chocolate spread. We just smiled at each other!'

WHAT YOU NEED
(makes 8 braaibroodjies)

16 slices white bread

butter (to spread on the bread)

1 jar Nutella (or similar chocolate hazelnut spread)

2 slabs (100 g each) **hazelnut chocolate** (roughly chopped)

1 cup pecan nuts (roughly chopped)

1 tsp ground cinnamon

whipped cream (to serve)

WHAT TO DO

1. Butter one side of each of the bread slices. The buttered sides will be the outsides of your braaibroodjies.
2. Pack half of the slices onto a cutting board, buttered side down, and cover with chocolate spread. Use a generous but reasonable amount of chocolate spread – not the whole jar.
3. Distribute the chopped chocolate and nuts onto the chocolate spread and then close each braaibroodjie with the remaining slices of bread, buttered sides facing upwards.
4. Place the braaibroodjies in a hinged grid and braai over medium heat, turning often until they're golden brown on the outside and the chocolate is melted on the inside.
5. Just before they are done, dust the braaibroodjies with ground cinnamon on both sides and toast a final minute or two.
6. Serve the chocolate braaibroodjies immediately with a side of whipped cream, or as is!

BREAKFAST BRAAI

BREAKFAST OF CHAMPIONS

This recipe is pretty self-explanatory and I trust that even the casual observer will clearly see how great it is by simply reading through it. You make a very high-quality relish in your potjie on the fire and then you poach some eggs in this relish. Simple as that.

WHAT YOU NEED
(feeds 4–6)

2 tots olive oil

1 red onion (sliced)

1 red pepper (sliced)

2 garlic cloves (crushed and chopped)

½ tsp cayenne pepper (or chilli powder)

1 tsp paprika

1 punnet (250 g) **cherry tomatoes** (halved)

1 tub (200 g) **feta cheese** (Danish style works best for this one)

6 jumbo eggs (the biggest eggs you can find)

salt and freshly ground pepper

handful of basil leaves (chopped or torn into smaller pieces)

bread slices (toasted on the fire, to serve)

WHAT TO DO

1. In your no. 10 flat-bottomed potjie, heat the oil, onion and pepper for a few minutes.
2. Add the garlic, cayenne pepper and paprika and fry for another minute.
3. Add the tomatoes and mix it all together. Let it simmer, covered with the lid, for about 10 minutes so that all the flavours can socialise and get to know each other.
4. Crumble all the feta evenly into the potjie on top of the tomato mixture.
5. Now use your wooden spoon and make six dents or hollows in the relish, big enough for an egg. Break an egg into each hole. And I mean break the shell and gently decant the actual egg into the relish, taking care not to break the egg yolks.
6. Season with salt and pepper and close the lid. Leave to cook for about 6 minutes on flames or coals. The relish needs to bubble as that will cook the eggs, so the heat can be high. The meal is ready when the egg whites are mostly cooked and the yellow still mostly soft. There is no harm in lifting the lid and peeking inside the potjie to see when and whether this is done.
7. Sprinkle with the basil leaves and serve immediately; this is not a meal that needs to rest before serving

AND …

Serve with fire-toasted bread or, for bonus points, roosterkoek (page 152).

BREAKFAST BRAAI MUESLI

When it comes down to it, a breakfast braai is just like any other braai later in the day; it just happens at sunrise. For a really impressive breakfast braai, you need to serve some really impressive things cooked on the fire. The thing about making your own muesli like this is that it looks and tastes better than anything store-bought, but more importantly, you can enjoy it hot off the fire!

WHAT YOU NEED
(feeds 4)

2 tots butter

2 cups oats

1 packet mixed nuts
(100 g, unsalted)

2 tots sunflower seeds

2 tots desiccated coconut

½ cup honey

juice of 1 orange

fresh fruit and plain yoghurt
(to serve)

WHAT TO DO

1. Heat the butter in your pot until bubbly, add the oats and stir so that all the oats are coated. Stir continuously so that the mixture does not burn, and toast for about 3 minutes.
2. Add the nuts, seeds and coconut and toast for another 2 minutes. Keep stirring the mixture while it is toasting until everything is brown and smelling great. If at any stage during the process you genuinely want to, you may add a bit more butter, but it's usually not necessary. Nuts burn much more easily than oats so pay attention. If there are a few unroasted nuts in your meal that is fine and perfect. If there are burnt ones it's not so ideal so err on the side of caution and rather halt the process sooner rather than later.
3. As the nuts get colour, drizzle the honey over everything and also add the orange juice. Stir the muesli with your wooden spoon, aiming to have an even distribution of the honey mixture. This will be a bit sticky, but just keep going as the honey will heat up and then spread more easily.
4. Once you're happy with the look and feel of the muesli, serve with fresh fruit and yoghurt.

BREAKFAST BRAAI OMELETTE

The bulk of this recipe was sent to me by Igna, who says her family often makes this meal on camping holidays. Their family calls it a breakfast pizza but as it's probably closer to an Italian frittata and its cousin the Spanish omelette, I went with the title you see here. As you might imagine, when you've done it once, this is a recipe you can use as a baseline for your own further experimentation with different ingredients.

WHAT YOU NEED
(feeds 6)

3 bell peppers (any combination of green, yellow or red, seeded and chopped)

1 large onion (chopped)

olive oil or butter

2 large tomatoes (chopped)

1 tot chutney

6 eggs (beaten)

1 tot milk

½ tsp salt

1 tsp ground black pepper

1 tsp dried oregano

roughly 200 g Cheddar cheese (grated)

fire-toasted bread or roosterkoek (to serve)

WHAT TO DO

1. In a pan on the fire, fry the chopped bell peppers and onion with olive oil or butter on high heat until things start to get personality.
2. Now add the tomatoes and chutney, and toss everything around for another few minutes until your mixture is well and truly stir-fried.
3. In rapid succession, add all of the eggs and milk, as well as the salt, pepper and oregano to the pan. Mix everything together so the egg mixture can fill the gaps between the rest of the ingredients and form a nice layer on top.
4. When things are evened out to your liking, top the eggs with all of the cheese and then close the pan with tight-fitting tinfoil. Let the pan stand over gentle heat for a few minutes until the egg is cooked and the cheese melted.
5. Serve with fire-toasted bread or freshly baked roosterkoek.

BRAAI TOAST

Dietitians agree that breakfast is one of the three most important meals of the day. Some even consider it the most important. We can never take matters of health too lightly and that is why it's important not only to prepare a proper breakfast but also to prepare it in the natural and original way – on a braai fire. The ingredients and steps of this recipe are all pretty straightforward and your meal should look and taste exactly like mine if you just follow the steps. The one ingredient to note is sour cream – something widely available in South Africa and something not sour at all. Commercially sold sour cream is actually pretty sweet and that is what you want for this meal. You can also use what is called 'crème fraîche', a product pretty much identical. I generally use preserved green figs for this number but when in season and available in your garden or at your local farm, market or supermarket, you can also be fancy and simply use fresh figs. Enjoy!

WHAT YOU NEED
(feeds 4)

1 cup pecan nuts
(roughly chopped)
4 eggs
½ cup milk
salt and pepper
8 slices white bread
butter (for frying)
**1 cup sour cream
or crème fraîche**
**1 cup preserved
green figs** (sliced)
honey (optional)

WHAT TO DO

1. Dry-roast the chopped pecan nuts in a pan and set aside for later use. Nuts in a very hot pan on the fire burn quickly so pay attention to this step and remove the nuts from the pan as soon as they start to brown.
2. Use a mixing bowl and a whisk or fork and mix the eggs and milk really well until everything is smooth and yellow. Season the mixture with salt and pepper.
3. Place a slice of bread into the egg mixture to soak and heat a teaspoon of butter in your fireproof pan. Place the soaked bread slice into your warm pan and let it toast on both sides until it has a nice rich brown colour and the egg is cooked. Now repeat this step with all the slices of bread.
4. To serve, spread one slice of bread with sour cream, place a few pieces of sliced fig and some roasted nuts on top, and cover with another slice of toast, also topped with sour cream, figs and nuts.
5. If it's your birthday, or any other day of the year, and you're feeling particularly decadent, top it off with a drizzle of honey.

AND ...

Naturally, when you prepare this meal at home you can just build separate two-slice portions on different plates for each person. We just built one massive stack like this for the photo in this book because it looks awesome!

PASTA & RISOTTO POTJIES

BUTTERNUT LASAGNE POTJIE

Lasagne is the first actual meal I learnt how to cook. My mother taught me the original recipe and, subjective as I am, it's one of my best and favourite recipes. Apart from the single change of swapping the meat for butternut here (which I often do at home as well, with great success) this is my signature lasagne.

WHAT YOU NEED
(feeds 4–6)

12 lasagne sheets

FOR THE MAIN SAUCE
1 tot butter

1 onion (finely chopped)

1 garlic clove (crushed and chopped)

1 cup mix of grated carrots and finely chopped celery

500 g butternut (peeled and diced into small blocks)

½ cup dry red wine

2 tins chopped tomatoes

1 tot tomato paste

1 tot dried oregano

1 bay leaf

1 tsp salt

1 tsp pepper

FOR THE BÉCHAMEL (WHITE) SAUCE
3 tots butter

3 tots white bread or cake flour

2 cups vegetable stock

½ cup cream

1 cup Cheddar cheese (or Parmesan, grated)

½ tsp nutmeg

salt and pepper

WHAT TO DO

1. Make the main sauce: In the pot that you will bake the lasagne in, heat the butter, add the onion, garlic, carrot and celery, and fry gently until soft. Some light flames should give you the correct heat. If it fries too rapidly, remove the pot from the flames and heat it with a few coals. Add the butternut and fry for 2–3 minutes. Then add the wine, tomatoes, tomato paste, oregano, bay leaf, salt and pepper. Stir very well then simmer for 15 or more minutes, stirring now and then, until the butternut goes soft. Keep the cooked sauce in another container until you need it for step 3.

2. Make the béchamel sauce: In a separate pot, melt the butter and use a wooden spoon to mix the flour completely into the melted butter. Now add the stock bit by bit while you continuously stir the mixture. When all the stock has been added, let the sauce simmer for a few minutes. Remove from the heat and stir in the cream, grated cheese and nutmeg. Add salt and pepper to taste.

3. Build the lasagne: Fill the cast-iron pot with layers of the main sauce, lasagne sheets and béchamel sauce. A flat-bottomed pot will result in a neater lasagne but any round-bottomed pot is also fine.

4. Put the lid on the pot and bake the lasagne for about 45 minutes by placing the pot on a stand over coals and also putting a few coals on the lid of the pot. When all the lasagne sheets are completely soft, the dish is ready.

BRANDY PASTA

In my second book, *Red Hot*, there is a recipe for a vodka pasta potjie – a fantastic recipe, except that it contains bacon and thus cannot be included in this vegetarian book. In my fourth book, *Shisanyama*, there is a recipe for a chorizo pasta potjie – again, very tasty but not suitable for a book that contains no meat. So I took the best bits of both those recipes and developed this one, which I am pretty sure fans of the original two recipes will love and which will also prove very popular with all the vegetarian readers of my books.

WHAT YOU NEED
(feeds 4–6)

500 g pasta (for this meal I prefer penne, but use what you like)

1 tot olive oil

1 tot butter

1 onion (very finely chopped)

2 garlic cloves (crushed and chopped)

1 fresh red chilli (chopped)

2 tins chopped tomatoes

½ tot sugar

1 tot balsamic vinegar

1 tsp salt

½ tsp pepper

1 cup cream

½ cup brandy

Parmesan cheese or mature Cheddar cheese (to serve)

fresh herbs (like basil or parsley, to serve)

WHAT TO DO

1. In your potjie on a fire, cook the pasta in salted water for 6 minutes, then drain it and keep it aside. The pasta won't be completely cooked but this is what you want, as it will be finished later.
2. Put the same (now empty) potjie back on the fire, heat the oil and butter, then fry the onion until soft but not too brown. Add the garlic and chilli and then fry for another minute.
3. Now add the chopped tomatoes, sugar, balsamic vinegar, salt and pepper. Stir well, then cover and simmer for 15 minutes until it gets thicker.
4. To add the cream to the meal without the risk of it curdling, decant it into a bowl. Now add a spoon of warm sauce from the potjie to the cream and stir that into the cream. Continue this process spoon by spoon until the cream mixture is warm. Now throw all of that into the potjie, stir well and bring it all to the boil.
5. As soon as it is boiling, add the half-cooked pasta from step 1 and pour in the brandy. Bring it to the boil again, then cook uncovered until the sauce thickens and the pasta starts to absorb the sauce.
6. Remove from the fire and serve. As with any tomato-based pasta, you can serve it with grated or shaved Parmesan or Cheddar cheese, and as with almost any pasta, tomato base or not, you can drizzle it with quality South African olive oil.
7. Serve with salt and pepper on the table, as well as some fresh herbs like basil or parsley.

MUSHROOM RISOTTO

Many people don't know, or believe me when I say, that there is an easier way to make risotto. Easier than the traditional Italian way that is. Gone are the days of standing there for hours, adding liquid, little by little, to the pot when I can already tell you how much liquid you need. I believe that life should be easier, so here you go. The mushroom risotto gets its flavour from the mushrooms so try to include a combination of mushroom options like white button or portabellini instead of just one type.

WHAT YOU NEED
(feeds 4)

1 tot olive oil

1 tot butter

1 onion (finely chopped)

2 garlic cloves (crushed and chopped)

500 g mushrooms (chopped)

½ cup white wine

4 cups vegetable stock (preferably liquid stock)

1 cup risotto rice

½ cup Parmesan cheese (or pecorino cheese)

salt and pepper (to taste)

fresh thyme (optional, to garnish)

WHAT TO DO

1. Light a big fire with your favourite braai wood.
2. Heat the oil and butter in your potjie by getting some flames under the potjie, then fry the onion for a few minutes. Now add the garlic and fry for about a minute or two.
3. Next, add the mushrooms and fry for a few minutes until soft. It will be a big heap of mushrooms, but will get smaller with time.
4. When you feel the moment is right, add the wine and stir so that everything can mix together. Stir until most of the alcohol cooks away. Now add the stock and bring the mixture to the boil.
5. Add the rice to the potjie, stir, and cover with a lid. Your temperature under the potjie should now be slightly approaching medium heat. You want a gentle simmer.
6. You should lift the lid regularly and stir the mixture to make sure nothing sticks to the bottom. In this case, 'regularly' means every 5 minutes. This step of simmering and stirring every 5 minutes is a really great task to delegate to other members of your braai gathering. That guest who asks if they can help? Let them do this. It will take about 30–40 minutes for the rice to be cooked.
7. The risotto is ready when the rice is thick and creamy and soft. In the highly unlikely event that the risotto goes dry and risks burning before the rice is soft, stir in a bit of water and use that to get yourself to the finish line.
8. Stir the cheese into the risotto and check the seasoning, adding salt and pepper if necessary.
9. Plate the risotto and top with extra cheese and fresh thyme.

SWEET POTATO PAELLA

Catering and kitchen shops sell a type of fireproof steel pan that is perfect for the preparation of this dish – so perfect, in fact, that this pan is widely referred to as a 'paella pan'. 'Paella' actually means 'pan' and this is where the name of the dish comes from. So it also does not necessarily need to contain fish – paella is just made in a pan. But you don't even need a pan for this paella – your favourite potjie will work absolutely fine and this is how I mostly do it at home.

WHAT YOU NEED
(feeds 6–8)

2 tots olive oil

1 onion

1 sweet bell pepper (green, red or yellow, chopped)

1 cup long-grain white rice (uncooked)

1 kg sweet potatoes (peeled and chopped into big chunks)

2 garlic cloves (crushed and chopped)

1 tsp paprika

1 tsp turmeric

½ tsp chilli powder

½ cup white wine

2 tomatoes (chopped)

2 cups vegetable stock

½ cup black olives (pitted)

250 g peas (they come in frozen packets of this size)

salt and pepper

parsley (to serve)

lemon wedges (to serve)

WHAT TO DO

1. In a large pan or potjie on the fire, fry the onion and pepper in the oil for 3 minutes. Your coals should be just hot enough to fry the onion. As the steel of a pan is much thinner than a cast-iron pot, it will be a bit more sensitive to heat.
2. Add the rice and mix well. All the rice should be thinly coated with oil. If this is not the case, add a bit more oil. Fry the rice for a few minutes until it turns pale golden in colour. Now add the sweet potato, garlic, paprika, turmeric, chilli powder, wine and chopped tomatoes, and stir-fry for another 2 minutes.
3. Add the stock and cover the pan with a lid or with tinfoil. The rice and sweet potato should now cook until soft, which will take about 40 minutes in total. Slightly reduce the heat under the pan by scraping away some coals. You are allowed to lift the lid now and again to stir the rice, and to monitor that it is not burning. Should everything seem a bit quiet, scrape a few extra coals back under the pan.
4. After 30 of those 40 minutes, add the olives and peas to the pan. Stir them in and cover the pan again for at least 10 minutes. Monitor your liquid level and add a bit more wine or water if the pan becomes too dry.
5. When the rice is soft and the sweet potato is cooked, sample the dish, add salt and pepper to taste, garnish with parsley and lemon wedges, and serve immediately.

AND ...

As with many great dishes cooked on a braai, paella ingredients are not exact. Take these ingredients as a guideline and make this recipe your own.

CAPER AND PECAN NUT PASTA

discovered this dish during a trip down the Amalfi Coast in Italy at a restaurant situated on a rocky beach in a small fishing village. In worse than broken Italian (a combination of grunts and sign language basically), I asked for whatever the chef considered his speciality dish. In front of my eyes, a fresh fish was carried from a boat into the restaurant and that same fish was on my table a little while later, with this pasta on the side. As with all my favourite Italian dishes, the ingredients are basic and the preparation simple. This dish originally contained anchovies, but it's presented here with capers, which have a similar depth of taste and saltiness. The recipe as it was shown to me in Italy also used walnuts, but pecan nuts are more widely available in South Africa. These are consequently more economically sensible and are close enough in taste, so that's what I always use.

WHAT YOU NEED
(feeds 4 as a light main meal)

1 cup (100 g) **pecan nuts**

500 g linguine or spaghetti

2 tots olive oil

2 tots capers

4 garlic cloves (crushed and chopped)

½ cup cream

2 tots parsley (chopped)

Parmesan (or pecorino cheese, to serve)

salt and pepper (to taste)

WHAT TO DO

1. Pound the nuts using a pestle and mortar. Alternatively, use a rolling pin or wine bottle to crush them finely on a chopping board.

2. Use a cast-iron pot to cook the pasta according to the instructions on the packet. This involves boiling water in a pot, adding salt to that water and cooking the pasta for roughly 8 minutes in the boiling water (but check the packaging as cooking times differ). If you are at the sea, use fresh seawater that already contains salt for this step. But not seawater with sand.

3. When the pasta is 90% done (just before al dente), remove from the pot, drain and set aside. Important: Save some of the water that you boiled the pasta in, as you will need this later.

4. Add olive oil to the now empty pot and fry the capers, garlic and nuts. Stir continuously and use a wooden spoon to press and mash the capers and garlic until they disintegrate and melt into the oil. This could happen as quickly as in 1 minute so keep a constant eye on the pot and don't try to multitask otherwise it will burn.

5. Steps 5 and 6 combined should take minutes you can count on one hand. Add the pasta to the caper-and-nut mixture in the pot and stir through. Add the cream and about half a cup of the water that you boiled the pasta in – just enough to create a bit of sauce and to keep the pasta from burning. Let that liquid boil and use a spoon or fork to toss the pasta around a bit. The amount of water you need to add will depend on the heat and the size and shape of your pot, so it might differ from one time to the next.

6. As soon as the pasta is heated through again and the sauce is thickened to your liking, stir in the parsley. The dish is now ready.

7. If the craving speaks to you, drizzle with high-quality South African olive oil. That craving often speaks to me.

8. Once it is served up, top the pasta with shavings of pecorino or Parmesan cheese. As the capers already added salt to the dish, let each guest add their own salt and pepper to taste.

BEAN BOLOGNESE

My family started making spaghetti Bolognese on the fire during camping trips in Botswana and Namibia when I was a teenager. The secret to a great Bolognese sauce is to simmer it over low coals for quite a while.

WHAT YOU NEED
(feeds 6)

2 tots olive oil

1 onion (finely chopped)

1 carrot (grated)

1 celery stick (finely chopped)

2 garlic cloves (crushed and chopped)

½ tot mixed dried herbs
(or 1 tot finely chopped fresh herbs like basil, thyme and parsley)

½ cup red wine

1 tin red kidney beans
(drained)

1 tin black beans (drained)

2 tins tomatoes

2 tots tomato paste

1 tsp sugar

½ tot lemon juice

salt (to taste)

ground black pepper
(to taste)

500 g pasta (like tagliatelle or spaghetti)

Parmesan cheese
(or Cheddar cheese, shaved or grated, to serve)

WHAT TO DO

1. Heat the oil in a potjie over a medium-hot fire. Add the onion, carrot and celery, and gently fry for 5–10 minutes until the onion is soft and shiny but not brown.
2. Add the garlic and herbs to the pot and fry for 2 minutes.
3. Pour in the wine and stir well. Use your spoon to scrape and loosen any bits stuck to the bottom of the pot. Cook until the wine is almost completely reduced.
4. Now add the beans, tomatoes, tomato paste, sugar, lemon juice, salt and pepper. Stir well and bring to a simmer over low heat. Put the lid on the pot and simmer for 1 hour, stirring every 10–15 minutes to ensure that the sauce doesn't cook dry and burn. You need low heat and a gentle simmer. If the pot runs dry, add a bit of water.
5. After 1 hour of cooking, add salt and pepper to taste. Take off the lid and simmer uncovered while you cook the pasta in salted water in a separate pot.
6. When the pasta is cooked and you're happy with the Bolognese sauce, serve as you see fit. I usually see fit with a bit of shaved Parmesan or grated aged white Cheddar.

AND ...

Pasta, like spaghetti and tagliatelle, takes about 7–8 minutes in plenty of rapidly boiling salted water to become al dente, which means 'just cooked with a slight bite to it'. For 500 g of pasta you need about 5 litres of water and ½ tot of salt. Don't overcook pasta or it will become a soggy mess. When it's done, drain the water off and immediately drizzle the pasta with olive oil to stop it sticking to itself.

GNOCCHI WITH BLUE CHEESE SAUCE

The inspiration for this recipe comes from Guido who, as you might guess from his name, is Italian. Guido once served me a brilliant blue cheese gnocchi – so brilliant that I had to go back the next day to have it again, and more importantly, learn how to make it myself.

WHAT YOU NEED
(feeds 6)

FOR THE GNOCCHI
1 kg (about 6) **potatoes** (peeled and chopped into chunks)

1 tsp salt

water

1 egg

2 cups white bread or cake flour

FOR THE SAUCE
1 tot butter

1 tot olive oil

2 onions (chopped)

2 garlic cloves (crushed and chopped)

1 cup cream

1 block (125 g) **blue cheese**

250 g white Cheddar cheese

fresh parsley (chopped, optional, to garnish)

WHAT TO DO

1. Cook the peeled potato chunks in salted water until very soft and they start cracking. Drain them and mash them very finely with a masher or a fork. Let the mashed potato cool down. It doesn't need to be ice cold – just cool enough that it doesn't cook the egg in the next step. We're talking about a cooling period in the region of half an hour, not half a day.
2. Add the egg to the cooled-down mashed potatoes and stir it in with a fork.
3. Now wash your hands, add 1 cup of flour and properly mix it into the mashed potatoes with a clean hand. Next, add the other cup of flour and mix that into the mashed potatoes as well.
4. Once you have a firm, soft piece of 'potato dough', take a ball or chunk of dough at a time and roll it into a sausage shape on a floured cutting board.
5. Cut these potato dough sausages into smaller pieces of about 2 cm each and gently roll each piece in flour. You need to coat each piece lightly in flour, otherwise they will all stick together.
6. Get a pot of water boiling on the fire to cook the gnocchi later.
7. Get another sizeable fireproof pan or a potjie on some flames and add the butter, oil and onion to that. Fry and toss the onion until you like the look of it and then add the garlic.
8. Soon after the garlic starts to brown, move the potjie or pan to an area with slightly less heat and add the cream, blue cheese and Cheddar cheese. Theoretically, you could grate the cheeses but that is actually too much work and just means you have to wash the grater. Simply use the same knife you used to chop the onion and garlic, and chop these cheeses into little blocks with that. Use a wooden spoon to stir everything. As soon as the cheese is in the pan, start cooking the gnocchi.
9. You will have to cook the gnocchi in batches. Add the gnocchi to the boiling pot of water you got going a while ago. The gnocchi will cook very quickly – in about a minute or two. Each individual piece will start to float on the surface as soon as it's ready.
10. Scoop the cooked gnocchi into a strainer, and from there into the pan with the sauce, or simply use a slotted spoon and take the pieces straight from the boiling water into the sauce.
11. Once all the gnocchi is united with the cheese sauce, gently toss everything so that all the pieces are coated with sauce and now let it simmer for a minute or two until you're happy with the look of it. In other words, until you've poured a few glasses of wine.
12. Serve garnished with parsley, or simply serve as is.

BUTTERNUT AND COCONUT MILK RISOTTO

Traditional pumpkin has all but disappeared from the South African pantry and there is a very good reason for that – butternut. The butternut is simply a superior member of the squash family. Traditional rice has all but disappeared from my kitchen as well. With curry potjies, I generally go for basmati or jasmine rice, and with all other potjies I mostly serve mashed potatoes or fresh bread. That is, when I am not making risotto!

Most of the ingredients are to some extent non-perishable, making this recipe perfect for two things: a backup option in your kitchen when the braai craving speaks to you unexpectedly, and secondly, a camping trip. Please note that I am aware that the method I use to make risotto is not what you see in old dusty cookbooks. I call it my method, the intelligent method or the modern method. No need for spoon-by-spoon liquid and a struggle. You're not an Italian in Italy in the 19th century. This is the modern world and there are easier ways to get to the same finish line.

WHAT YOU NEED
(feeds 4)

1 butternut (600 g when peeled and grated)

1 tot olive oil

1 tot butter

1 onion (finely chopped)

2 garlic cloves (crushed and chopped)

2 cups vegetable stock

1 cup white wine

1 tin coconut milk

1 cup risotto rice

salt and pepper (to taste)

fresh coriander (optional, to garnish)

100 g Parmesan or pecorino cheese (grated or shaved, optional, to serve)

WHAT TO DO

1. Peel your butternut, cut it open and remove the pips and other untoward stuff clinging to the inside. Now grate the butternut using the coarser side of your grater. It's absolutely fine not to grate that very last bit of butternut, as you might then destroy one or more of your fingertips on the grater and that is never ideal.

2. Heat the oil and butter in your potjie by getting some flames under it, and fry the onion for a few minutes. Now add the garlic and the grated butternut, and stir-fry for a couple more minutes.

3. Add the vegetable stock, all at once – yes, everything can go in at the same time. Also add the white wine and coconut milk. Stir until everything is combined, then bring to the boil.

4. Now add the cup of rice, all of it, and stir that in well. It will sink to the bottom of the potjie – don't panic. Place the lid on the pot. You should now have medium heat under your pot.

5. Lift the lid and stir regularly to make sure that the rice sinking to the bottom of the potjie does not buy a plot there, stick to it and burn. 'Regularly' in this case means stirring every 5 minutes and it is a really great task to delegate to other members of your braai party. Total cooking time for the rice to go soft will be about 30–40 minutes.

6. The risotto is ready when the rice is thick and creamy and soft. The butternut will be soft and fully cooked by that time as well. Should you run out of stock and coconut milk before the rice is completely soft (that is, you are scared it burns before it's soft), use a bit of water to get you to the finish line.

7. Flavour to taste with salt and pepper. Be very careful with the salt as the stock has already contributed salt to the meal.

8. Serve with some fresh coriander and, optionally, some cheese.

PUTTANESCA PASTA IN A POTJIE

Some people could have long debates on whether a recipe like this belongs in a braai book. The fact of the matter is that, to my mind, something delicious prepared in a cast-iron pot over an open fire is much closer to the essence of braaing than grilling a steak on a gas braai.

Puttanesca pasta is one of the true Italian classics, and something you really should master. The dish can be made entirely from non-perishable ingredients, making it a great meal to prepare when out on a camping trip or safari. This can be served as a light lunch or dinner on its own. The original recipe has anchovies, but I have replaced these with some extra capers, which to my mind have a similar enough depth of taste. So if you're a pescatarian, halve the capers and add a few anchovies!

WHAT YOU NEED
(feeds 4)

500 g spaghetti
water
1 tot salt
2 tots olive oil
2 big onions (chopped)
4 garlic cloves (crushed and chopped)
1 red chilli (seeded and chopped)
2 tots capers (drained)
1 cup black olives (drained and pitted)
2 tins peeled and chopped tomatoes
2 tots tomato paste
salt and pepper (to taste)
1 tot fresh parsley (chopped)
basil leaves (to garnish)

WHAT TO DO

1. Cook the pasta by placing the pot on the fire and bringing 4 litres of water to the boil. Add 1 tot of salt to this (yes, this is really necessary but don't worry; most of this salt will be thrown away with the water). Only add the pasta when the water is boiling properly. Spaghetti takes about 8 minutes to cook al dente, but you will have to check the packaging of the brand you are using and monitor its progress in the pot. You want to remove the pasta and drain it in a colander when it is 80% done.
2. Add the olive oil and chopped onion to the empty pot and return it to the fire. Lightly fry the onion for about 4 minutes.
3. Add the garlic and chilli, and fry for another 2 minutes.
4. Add the capers, olives, tomatoes and tomato paste. Stir well and simmer this sauce for about 20 minutes, stirring occasionally.
5. Add ground pepper and salt to taste. Go easy on the salt as the capers and olives already add saltiness to the pot.
6. Add the spaghetti and parsley, and toss together well until everything is properly mixed and the pasta is heated again.
7. Dish up straight from the pot and garnish with fresh basil.

AND ...

- You can obviously use other pasta as well but I like spaghetti.
- You can also use two different pots but I prefer this method as it means there is less to clean afterwards.
- The pasta will cook a bit more when it's added to the sauce again and, as cast iron retains its heat for a while, it will also continue to cook even after the pot is removed from the fire before you serve up. That is why you want to remove the pasta from the water before it is completely cooked.
- Keep some of the water you used to boil the pasta in. If the dish gets too dry when you add the pasta again at the end (if your fire is very hot and your pot lost too much moisture) then add some of this liquid instead of plain water.

BRAAIED MUSHROOM AND BASIL PESTO PASTA

The effort-to-impressive ratio of your own freshly made basil pesto is quite high as it looks cool, tastes great, has many uses and is very straightforward to make. There is also a wide margin for error, which is always a good thing, and when adding the ingredients, you can throw in more than the indicated amount of any ingredient (apart from the salt and pepper, that is) and the meal will just taste more strongly of that, without any risk whatsoever of spoiling what you're doing.

Braaing mushrooms – the other part of this recipe – is also very easy, which means that you can assemble quite a fancy meal by just systematically going through some easy motions. The toughest part is cooking the pasta, which isn't particularly challenging either.

WHAT YOU NEED
(feeds 4)

FOR THE BASIL PESTO
2 punnets (about 40 g) **fresh basil leaves**

2 garlic cloves (crushed and chopped)

100 g almonds or cashew nuts (raw or toasted)

100 g Parmesan cheese (or some similar hard and aged cheese, chopped or grated)

4 tots olive oil

1 tsp salt

½ tsp black pepper

FOR THE REST
400 g big brown mushrooms (whole)

250 g white button or brown portabellini mushrooms

olive oil (for serving)

skewers

500 g pasta of your choice

WHAT TO DO

1. To make the pesto, add all the ingredients together and use a food processor or stick blender to process it to a chunky paste. If you like olive oil (like me), add more of it when you feel the urge. Taste, and add a bit of salt and pepper as needed. The exact amount of salt and pepper will depend on the cheese, oil and basil you use. You can also use an old-fashioned pestle and mortar to work the ingredients into a paste and make the pesto. If you go this route, chop the basil leaves and garlic quite finely beforehand. Also use coarse salt flakes instead of normal fine table salt to make the grinding process a bit easier.

2. To braai the mushrooms, lightly brush the mushrooms with olive oil and then braai. Skewer button mushrooms but braai bigger mushrooms as is on a grid. Either way, putting the mushrooms in a hinged grid makes turning them easier. Braaing mushrooms takes about 6–10 minutes.

3. Cook the pasta according to the instructions on the packet. This usually involves boiling it in salted water for about 8 minutes. Drain the pasta and mix in the pesto. At this stage, I usually drizzle some additional olive oil onto the mixture.

4. Slice the mushrooms into strips or chunks and add them to the now-green pasta. Finish the work of art with a drizzle of your best South African olive oil.

AND ...

I specify the mushroom ingredients in this recipe to the gram as these are the pack sizes for mushrooms in South Africa at the time of writing this book. Do not overthink slight variations – just use packs of whatever weights are in the ballpark.

TOMATO RISOTTO

For our next magic trick, we combine all the flavours found in a classic Caprese meal. Strong tomato flavours, creamy cheese and fresh basil. Risotto is a wonderful blank canvas to play around with on the fire, especially since various different combinations of flavours tend to work well in a potjie. As with any potjie, you usually start by frying onions in oil, or butter, or both. You then start layering your flavour profile and in the case of risotto, it comes down to ending up with just more than a litre of liquid per cup of rice you intend adding. So essentially the first phase involves making a flavourful 'soup' in the potjie.

Once this 'soup' tastes exactly right, you add the risotto rice and let it simmer for just more than half an hour until the rice is soft and creamy. Remove the lid and stir every few minutes during this time so that nothing sticks and burns at the bottom. Spend the rest of the time relaxing, drinking wine and deciding what you're dressing the meal with once plated. It really is as simple as that.

WHAT YOU NEED
(feeds 4)

2 tots olive oil

2 onions (chopped)

2 garlic cloves (crushed and chopped)

50 g tomato paste

1 tin tomatoes (chopped or cherry)

500 ml vegetable stock

1 cup wine (red or white or rosé)

1 tsp salt

1 tsp pepper

1 tsp dried mixed herbs

1 cup risotto rice

1 tsp sugar (optional)

1 cup cream

1 cup Cheddar cheese (grated)

fresh basil (to serve)

WHAT TO DO

1. Heat the oil in your potjie and fry the onion and garlic for a few minutes.
2. Add the tomato paste, tomatoes, vegetable stock, wine, salt, pepper and herbs, and mix well. Let this soup simmer for 10 minutes for the flavours to develop. Taste it – if you feel it needs anything more, add that.
3. Now add the cup of risotto rice, stir, and cover with the lid.
4. Let this pot simmer for 30–40 minutes until the risotto is thick and creamy and all the liquid is absorbed. You have to lift the lid every few minutes to stir everything well and prevent the rice from sticking to the bottom of the potjie.
5. This step is optional, as is the sugar. Not all stock and especially not all tins of tomato are created equal. Some are more sweet and some are less sweet. As the cooking is nearing the end, taste the risotto, and frequently but not always you will find it is not quite sweet enough and needs a little sugar. If that's the case, stir in a teaspoon of sugar, but if you find the risotto to be sweet enough already, which will most likely be the case if the tomatoes you used were in fact sweet enough, then do not add any extra sugar.
6. When you are happy with the consistency of the risotto, meaning the rice is soft and the texture as a whole is creamy, add the cream and the cheese, and stir so that all the flavours can mix together. Now you can cruise to the finish line for a final few minutes and the feast is ready to enjoy!
7. Serve drizzled with olive oil and topped with fresh basil.

MACARONI AND CHEESE POTJIE

People refer to certain meals as 'comfort food', which is strange because I find eating most foods comforting. Nonetheless, some foods are more comforting than others, with a macaroni and cheese potjie right up there. You can either serve this as a main course, or as a very impressive side dish.

WHAT YOU NEED

(feeds 4–6)

500 g macaroni

2 tots olive oil

2 tots butter

2 tots white bread or cake flour

1 litre (4 cups) milk

400 g mature Cheddar cheese (grated)

1 heaped tsp Dijon mustard

1 tsp salt

1 tsp black pepper

a little bit of ground nutmeg (optional)

200 g feta cheese (crumbled)

fresh green herb of your choice (like basil, chives, spring onions or rocket, chopped)

WHAT TO DO

1. In a big enough potjie over a hot fire, bring water with about half a tot of salt to boiling point. Add all of the macaroni to the bubbling water and cook for about 8 minutes until almost done. You want the pasta slightly undercooked, as it will continue cooking later in the sauce. Drain off all water immediately and drizzle with the olive oil to prevent the macaroni from sticking together.

2. Return the empty potjie to the fire (not too hot), then add butter and wait until it melts. Add the flour and stir for about 1 minute.

3. Now add the milk, bit by bit, stirring continuously. You will notice how the butter and flour mixture first grows and absorbs all the milk you add, and how this thick paste then starts turning into a sauce as you add more and more milk. If you add the milk too quickly, lumps will form. If at any time you notice lumps forming, first stir them vigorously into the rest of the mixture before adding more milk.

4. When all the milk is in, bring the sauce to a slow simmer and add the cheese, mustard, salt and pepper (and nutmeg), and stir well.

5. Now add the cooked macaroni to the sauce, stir to coat the pasta well, then remove the potjie from the fire.

6. Crumble the feta cheese on top of the meal in the potjie, close the lid and let it sit until serving time.

7. Right before serving, chop your green herbs. Remove the lid of the potjie and sprinkle the chopped herbs on top of the feta cheese.

AND ...

The quality and taste of the cheese used will influence the end product. For a recipe like this, I would suggest using Cheddar that has been aged for at least 3 months. Using more mature Cheddar or even a variety of mature cheeses like Cheddar, Parmesan, pecorino, Gruyère and blue cheese will increase the depth of flavour.

VEGETABLES

CHERMOULA MIELIES

Widely available, photogenic, lasts quite well in your fridge, tasty, best done on the braai. Ticks all the boxes.

WHAT YOU NEED
(feeds 4)

4 mielies (corn)

FOR THE CHERMOULA
3 tots olive oil
3 garlic cloves (crushed and chopped)
1 lemon (juice)
2 tots fresh coriander (chopped)
2 tots parsley (chopped)
1 tsp paprika
1 tsp cumin powder
1 tsp ground coriander
1 tsp salt

WHAT TO DO

1. Make the sauce by combining all the ingredients in a food processor, or pestle and mortar.
2. If the mielies still have husk on them, remove it.
3. Now pack the mielies side by side on a braai grid and braai over hot coals for about 10 minutes, turning them during this time and exposing all sides to the heat of the coals.
4. When they are starting to look nicely browned, remove the mielies from the fire and generously lather each one with chermoula sauce.
5. Now it's back to the fire to toast the mielies and sauce for a few minutes. You want the sauce to heat up and caramelise here and there.
6. Once you feel it's ready, you're right – it's ready. Remove from the fire and serve immediately. If there is still sauce left over and you feel like it, drizzle that over the mielies.

AND ...

Sometimes, when the food chain from farmer to you is quite short, you'll get hold of mielies that are still completely in the husk. In this case, consider braaing them directly on the coals exactly as they come, turning them now and then. They will steam, cook and braai perfectly just like that. As soon as a kernel starts to show through the husk – that is, when the leaves start to burn away in some parts – that mielie is ready to be eaten. Remove from the fire, remove all the husk and enjoy as is or dressed with the sauce.

BRAAIED SWEET PEPPER SALAD

Preparing braaied or charred peppers on the fire is very easy and once done they are like a utility back in a rugby team – quite versatile. There are a few reasons why it's a good idea to braai or, more accurately, char peppers. It makes the process easier to separate the tough skin from the silky flesh of sweet peppers. They also become even sweeter through the process of caramelisation. It makes them softer. And it gives them a smoked fire taste. In summary, braaing peppers transforms them from good to great.

WHAT YOU NEED
(feeds 4)

3 bell peppers (1 red, 1 yellow, 1 green)

½ cup pumpkin seeds

200 g baby spinach leaves (this is not an exact science; use more if you are rabbit-like and fond of leaves)

1 tin chickpeas (drained and washed under cold running water)

1 red onion (sliced thinly)

1 cup pitted olives

a few basil leaves (torn)

1 tub feta cheese (200 g, drained and crumbled)

2 tots olive oil

1 lemon (juice)

2 tots balsamic vinegar

salt and pepper

WHAT TO DO

1. Place the peppers on a grid, or skewer them on your grandfather's sword from the war and suspend them over flames until blackened on all sides. You will obviously need to turn them now and again to expose all sides to the flames.
2. Once blackened on all sides, place the peppers into a plastic bag, close the bag and leave for 20 minutes to cool down.
3. While you wait, roast the pumpkin seeds in a dry pan over a hot fire for a few minutes until they start to smell fantastic. Here and there they will also start to pop. Immediately remove from the pan and let them wait somewhere tranquil like in a bowl, plate or mug.
4. Peel the skins off the peppers (they will come off easily) and cut them open. Scrape out and discard all the unsavoury innards and seeds, and then cut the flesh into chunky blocks. Here and there you will have bits of charred skin left on the flesh. This is fine and part of the final flavour.
5. Place the spinach in a bowl and add the charred pieces of pepper, chickpeas, red onion, olives and basil, and mix everything together.
6. Sprinkle the roasted pumpkin seeds and crumbled feta over the salad.
7. Dress with high-quality South African olive oil, lemon juice and balsamic vinegar, and season with salt and pepper.

COAL-BAKED POTATO AND ONION WITH MUSHROOM SAUCE

WHAT YOU NEED
(feeds 4-6)

6 medium-to-large potatoes

tinfoil

6 onions

FOR THE SAUCE

500 g mushrooms (finely chopped)

1 tot olive oil

1 cup cream

salt and pepper

1 egg

250 g (1 tub) **plain cream cheese** (I prefer full fat)

WHAT TO DO

1. Wash the potatoes in or under cold water and then wrap each potato tightly in tinfoil. No need to dry them carefully – just wrap them up.
2. Peel and wrap the onions in foil. Add a little butter, garlic butter, olive oil, balsamic vinegar or wine to each onion before you wrap it up.
3. Take the potatoes and onions to the fire immediately. I usually place them at the edge of my fire and then position the odd coal around and on top of them. When the fire has burnt out and the coals are spread open, just put them all along the border of your circle of coals.
4. Assuming your fire takes about 40 minutes to burn out and your braai another 10–20 minutes, the potatoes will be done by the time you have finished braaing. Onions are a little quicker – roughly 30 minutes. As such you can just move them slightly further away from the brunt of the coals once they feel soft and done. To test whether the potatoes are done, press on each one with your tongs and if they are soft and yielding, you know that they are ready; alternatively, pierce the potato with a knife through the foil and check whether the knife goes in easily. Remember that not all of them will take exactly the same time, as their positioning in the coals will make a difference.
5. Using tongs, remove the potatoes and onions from the fire and shake off all the ash.
6. Cut a cross into the top of each potato through the tinfoil using a large knife.
7. Use your thumbs and forefingers to press each potato from four sides so that the top opens like a flower.
8. Unwrap the onions and serve with the potatoes.
9. Spoon some mushroom sauce on top of the potatoes and onions.

TO MAKE THE SAUCE

1. Fry the chopped mushrooms in the oil until soft.
2. Add the cream, salt and pepper, and bring to the boil.
3. Beat the egg and then add about half a cup of the warm cream-and-mushroom mix to the egg, stirring continuously.
4. Now add this egg mix back to the rest of the mushroom cream in the pot.
5. Stir in the cream cheese until everything is combined; heat until it simmers.

AND ...

- If you're feeling lazy, leave out the egg.
- The cream cheese can be replaced with any normal cheese like Cheddar or Gouda – just grate it before stirring it in.
- There's nothing stopping you from adding a glass of white wine to this sauce. It is a well-known fact that white wine complements mushrooms, cream and cheese.

BUTTERNUT WITH A FILLING

This dish is the fancy cousin of the potato baked in foil. It is incredibly simple to prepare yet never fails to impress people who are not used to it.

WHAT YOU NEED
(each butternut feeds 2)

butternuts
filling of your choice (see below)
a roll of tinfoil

FILLING (choose one)
creamed spinach and mushroom (made by lightly frying mushroom and chopped spinach and mixing that with cream cheese)
garlic and herb butter (made by mixing garlic, herbs and butter)
onion, pepper and feta (fry onion and sweet pepper, then mix with crumbled feta)
sweetcorn (made by opening a tin of sweetcorn or creamed sweetcorn)

WHAT TO DO

1. Do not peel the butternuts!
2. Slice each butternut in half using a big, sharp knife. Use a spoon to scrape out the pips and strings from the cavity.
3. Load the cavities with the filling of your choice.
4. Tightly wrap each butternut in tinfoil and pack them on coals at the edge of the heat zone of your fire. Position a few coals around and on top of each butternut. To cook them evenly, rotate the butternuts occasionally or move and adjust the coals.
5. They are done when their flesh yields under the foil when you press them with braai tongs. This should take about 40 minutes. Alternatively, insert a knife into them through the foil and if the knife goes in easily they are ready. Each guest gets half a butternut and can open the foil themselves to see and smell the aroma of the steam as it escapes.

AND ...

Try and get nice small butternuts so that half a butternut can be served to each person. Bigger butternuts also work, but they will take closer to an hour to cook and you might have to slice them up further before serving, which does not look as attractive on a plate.

SOETPATAT

A bit of background on the soetpatat. In Afrikaans, my first language and the most commonly spoken language up the West Coast, sweet potato is called patat. When slices of patat are fried and stewed with butter, sugar and a bit of cinnamon we call it soetpatat, which translates to 'sweet sweet potato'. It's an outstanding dish as is but also goes very well with and is the classic side dish to serve with braaied snoek. I know this is a vegetarian book, but for the pescatarians, have this one with fish!

WHAT YOU NEED
(feeds 4–6)

1 cup honey (or sugar)

½ cup butter

1 cinnamon stick

peel of ¼ of an orange

1 tsp salt

1 kg sweet potato (peeled and sliced, or cut into chunks)

WHAT TO DO

1. Heat the honey (or sugar) and butter in a pot. Mix well and when it is all melted, add the cinnamon stick, orange peel, salt and sweet potato slices or chunks.
2. Stir and mix it all together and then put the lid on the pot. Gently simmer with the lid on for about 30 minutes until all the sweet potatoes are soft. During this time you can use a large spoon or spatula to toss the mixture very gently once or twice. Do not remove the lid at any other stage and do not stir more often. Creating mash will taste the same but is not considered stylish.
3. Serve immediately while nice and warm.

AUBERGINE

The aubergine goes by many names and I usually call it a brinjal; but considering that the spell checker of the word-processing program that I used to type this book did not think that brinjal was a word, I went with aubergine for the heading. Another name often used for this vegetable is eggplant. The brinjal has as many uses on the braai as it has names. Brinjal skins can be eaten and you don't need to peel them for any of the recipes below.

WHAT YOU NEED

FOR THE CHIPS
brinjals
course sea salt
olive oil (optional)

FOR THE SIDE DISH
brinjals
salt
olive oil

FOR THE SALAD
brinjals
1 pepper (red, yellow or green, chopped)
1 onion (chopped)
2 cloves garlic (crushed and chopped)
olive oil
4 big tomatoes (or a host of cherry tomatoes, chopped)
2 feta cheese wheels (chopped)
salt
chilli powder
fresh basil or parsley (to garnish)

MAKE CHIPS

1. Thinly slice each brinjal lengthwise and lie the slices on a clean surface. Now salt each slice with a bit of coarse sea salt. The salt will draw out some water and assist you in the mission of making crisp chips.
2. When the fire is burnt out and the coals are ready, shake or scrape off all the salt and dry each slice with paper towel. Braai each slice for a minute or two on both sides on hot coals. Each slice takes quite a bit of braai-grid space so you might need more than one grid or you'll have to do the braai in batches. If you want to make the effort, paint the slices with olive oil during the braai.
3. Serve the brinjal chips to guests around the braai.

MAKE A SIDE DISH

Slice each brinjal in thicker slices of about 1 cm each and grind salt onto them. Leave until the coals are ready, then shake or scrape off the salt and pat dry with paper towel. Braai over medium heat until browned and soft. Paint with olive oil during the braai. Serve as a side dish.

MAKE A SALAD

1. Braai thicker slices of brinjal as described above and remove from the fire when ready. Brinjal slices physically change colour as they cook – similar to onions. When you braai them you will see what I mean. When all the white is gone, they are ready.
2. Cut each slice into squares of about 2 cm × 2 cm.
3. Fry the pepper, onion and garlic in a bit of olive oil for a minute or 3.
4. Put the tomatoes and feta cheese in a bowl, and add the fried mixture.
5. Mix all of the above together and drizzle this salad with olive oil. Add salt and chilli powder to taste and garnish with fresh basil or parsley.

AWESOME IDEAS

CREAMY GARLIC MUSHROOMS (ON TOAST)

'm a big fan of mushrooms, onions, garlic and cream as individuals. Together they create an exquisite taste, or as Aristotle used to say, 'the whole is greater than the sum of its parts'. It's a nice starter or side dish and is also known to be very popular around the late-night 'atmosfire' as a second braai of the evening.

WHAT YOU NEED
(feeds 4–6 as a snack)

2 tots butter

1 tot olive oil

1 onion (chopped)

4 cloves garlic
(crushed or chopped)

500 g whole mushrooms
(brown, button or any
mixture of these or others
sold commercially for culinary
consumption)

1 sprig thyme (stalk removed)

1 tsp salt

½ tsp black pepper

1 cup cream (250 ml tub)

slices of bread
(toasted – optional, to serve)

1 tot finely chopped parsley
(optional, to serve)

WHAT TO DO

1. Heat the oil and butter in a potjie or flameproof pan over a hot fire, add the chopped onion and fry until they become very soft and begin to turn light brown on the edges. Depending on your heat, this will take about 5 minutes.
2. Add the garlic, mushrooms and thyme, then fry until the mushrooms soften and start to brown (your pan needs to be very hot so don't be shy about having a few flames under it). Initially, the mushrooms might struggle to fit into the pan, but they will shrink as they cook.
3. Season with salt and pepper, then pour over the cream and bring to the boil. Simmer the cream for a few minutes, stirring often, until it reduces and forms a thick sauce (it'll darken slightly and turn a shade of grey, like the mushrooms). Timing is pretty important. You need to remove the potjie or pan from the fire when the sauce is thick, but before it has reduced too much and all the sauce is gone. If you don't have time to reduce the whole cup of cream, just use half a cup, but be aware that the meal won't taste quite as awesome.
4. Use a large spoon to scoop the creamy mushrooms onto the toasted bread and serve immediately, topped with finely chopped parsley.

AND …

The quality of bread used has a direct impact on the end result and your enjoyment of the meal. These days we have a wide variety of great breads available in South Africa and, compared with meat, special breads are relatively cheap so buy the best available. When you walk into an artisan bakery and you feel a bit unsure of yourself, just ask for a sourdough bread. Bunny chow (see page 120) is the exception to the rule; for that, you're supposed (obliged) to use stock-standard white supermarket bread.

When serving braaied food with a slice of bread, you want to butter the bread on one side and toast it over medium coals for the final few minutes of your braai until golden brown. The idea is to have it ready with the rest of the meal.

For any braaied meal in this book that I suggest you serve with bread, you get bonus points if you serve it with freshly braaied roosterkoek, but I'm not going to mention it on every page as this would insult your intelligence.

BRATKARTOFFELN – THE GERMAN CLASSIC

Bratkartoffeln is to Germans what French fries are to Americans. The trick is to pan-fry cooked potatoes, and the more heat you have in your pan, the easier this is. As such, the best way to prepare bratkartoffeln is in a pan over the flames of a wooden fire.

WHAT YOU NEED
(feeds 6 as a side dish)

1 kg potatoes
2 tots oil (vegetable or olive)
2 tots butter
1 onion (finely chopped)
1 red bell pepper (seeded and sliced)
1 tot paprika
2 tots parsley (chopped)
salt and black pepper

WHAT TO DO

1. Do not peel the potatoes yet. Boil them in their skins until just before they are done (that is, tender but still firm). This will take about 20 minutes and can be done hours in advance or even the previous day. Remove from the water and let them cool down slightly for 10 minutes.
2. Peel the potatoes. No need for a potato peeler – just pull the skins off with the aid of a knife.
3. Now let the potatoes cool down completely. You can even store them in a fridge during this time.
4. Cut the boiled, peeled potatoes into slices 5 mm (½ cm) thick. Alternatively, cut into small cubes.
5. Use a large steel pan, add half of the oil and butter to it and fry the potato pieces for a few minutes on all sides until they start turning golden brown. You need a large pan so as to expose all the potatoes to the bottom of the pan and thus get them 'frying' instead of 'steaming'. If your pan is not big enough, split all the ingredients in half and perform steps 5, 6 and 7 twice.
6. Add the onion, peppers and the rest of the oil and butter to the pan, and continue to fry the whole lot until the onions are golden and translucent.
7. Now add the paprika and continue to fry everything until the potatoes are nicely browned and crispy. You want to be careful when turning the potatoes, as the idea is to create this dish without breaking or mashing too many of them. A large spatula works best.
8. Finally, add the parsley and season generously with salt and black pepper to taste.

SPANAKOPITA

Spanakopita, the classic Greek dish, can be braaied very successfully by using mild coals and a hinged grid. Needless to say, you serve the spanakopita with crisp white wine or grappa. Opa!

WHAT YOU NEED
(feeds 6–10)

600 g spinach (I prefer baby spinach)

1 onion (finely chopped)

1 tot olive oil

200 g feta (1 small tub)

2 eggs (lightly beaten)

1 tsp salt

1 tsp black pepper

2 packets (400 g each) **puff pastry** (defrosted)

WHAT TO DO

1. Fresh spinach generally contains a fair amount of soil. Rinse thoroughly to get rid of any grittiness, and dry to get rid of excess water. Chop the spinach a bit with your sharpest, newest, most prized knife.

2. Using your biggest pan, fry the onion in the oil until it's soft and starts to turn golden brown. Add the spinach. You may find that you struggle to fit all the spinach in, but as soon as it starts to cook, the spinach will wilt down to a fraction of its original size. Let the spinach cook for a few minutes until all the excess moisture has cooked off. If you have one, you can also do this step on a stove. The spanakopita will get its braai taste later on anyhow. Take it off the heat and add the fried spinach and onion to a large mixing bowl.

3. Crumble the feta into the mixing bowl, then add the eggs, salt and pepper. Mix well.

4. Unroll the puff pastry and dust each sheet lightly with flour on one side – the side that you'll use on the outside. This will stop the pastry sticking to the grid. If you don't have any flour on hand, you could lightly oil the grid.

5. Gently put one sheet of puff pastry onto the inside of a hinged grid. Spoon the filling evenly over the sheet, leaving a border of about 2 cm empty. Brush this edge with some water.

6. Now put the second sheet on top of the filled bottom layer. Use your hands to press the edges carefully together so that it seals (the water you painted onto the edges helps them to stick together). Use a knife or fork to prick a few small holes into the pie so that steam can escape while it is cooking.

7. Carefully close the grid, then braai the spanakopita over a medium fire with the grid fairly high for about 20–30 minutes until it is golden brown and cooked. Your only risk is burning the pastry, so rather go too slow than too fast. As you braai, lift the top half of the grid off the surface of the pastry every time you turn the grid to make sure the pastry doesn't rise or bake into the grid.

8. When it is ready, carefully take the trophy off the grid and put it onto a wooden chopping board. Slice into squares or triangles.

BOBOTIE

Bobotie is a South African classic and an important part of our culinary heritage. It's also one of my favourite meals, but this doesn't make me special: everybody loves bobotie. As with many other South African cult hits, the best and original way is in a potjie on a braai fire. I believe it's your moral duty to perfect the art of making bobotie. It's a great way to show off when you cook for visitors to South Africa. And here you have a version that is vegetarian.

WHAT YOU NEED
(feeds 6)

500 g lentils (I like the multicoloured pack but any will do)

2 tots olive oil

3 onions (finely chopped)

3 garlic cloves (crushed and chopped)

1 tot medium-strength curry powder

½ tot ground turmeric

½ tot salt

1 tsp black pepper

1 cup apricot jam

½ cup raisins

½ cup almond flakes

1 tot vinegar (or lemon juice)

3 eggs

1 cup milk

5 bay leaves

2 cups uncooked rice (to serve – this is usually spot-on for 6 people once cooked)

chutney (to serve)

WHAT TO DO

1. Place the lentils in your potjie on the fire with enough water to cover them, and simmer until soft for about 20 minutes. Drain and keep aside.
2. Heat the oil in a flat-bottomed potjie over a medium-hot fire and fry the onions and garlic until the onions are soft but not brown.
3. Add the curry powder and turmeric, then fry for a minute – the bottom of the potjie will look quite dry so pay attention and don't let the mixture burn.
4. Add the cooked lentils and fry for a few minutes, mixing everything together.
5. Add the salt and pepper, apricot jam, raisins, almond flakes and vinegar/lemon juice. Stir well, bring to a slow simmer and put on the lid. Simmer for about 10 minutes, stirring once in a while to make sure the mixture doesn't burn.
6. Now remove the lid and flatten the mixture with the back of your spoon so that it's even across the bottom of the potjie. Whisk the eggs and milk together in a small mixing bowl, then pour over the bobotie. Stick the bay leaves into the egg mixture. Cover with the lid and put a layer of hot coals on top of the lid. At this stage, you only want coals on the lid, not underneath the potjie. Bake like this for 30 minutes and then your bobotie is ready.
7. Serve with rice and chutney on the side.

AND ...

Many seasoned bobotie eaters also like sliced banana, coconut or chopped tomatoes with their bobotie. Serve whichever sambals you prefer.

UMNGQUSHO

Umngqusho is a traditional Xhosa dish made with samp (stamp mielies) and beans – one of Nelson Mandela's favourites. One of my favourites as well to be honest. Samp needs to soak in water overnight, so remember to start the day before.

WHAT YOU NEED
(feeds 8–10)

THE DAY BEFORE
500 g samp and bean mix
water

ON THE DAY
1 tot olive oil
1 onion (finely chopped)
2 carrots (peeled and chopped)
2 potatoes (peeled and chopped)
1 tot mild curry powder
2 litres water
1 litre vegetable stock
1 tin chopped tomatoes
50 g sachet onion soup powder (brown or white)
salt (optional, to taste)
1 cup Cheddar cheese (grated)

WHAT TO DO

1. Add the samp and bean mix to any suitably sized container and add water until the samp and beans are covered. Now let the samp and beans soak in the water overnight.
2. The next day when you're ready for action, drain the water off and rinse the samp and beans well.
3. In a large potjie, add the oil, onion, carrots and potatoes and fry for a few minutes until the onion looks like you feel it should look.
4. Now add the curry powder, toss around over heat for another minute and then rapidly proceed to the next step.
5. Add the soaked samp and beans, 2 litres of water (adding boiling water makes it all go a bit quicker), the vegetable stock and the tin of chopped tomatoes.
6. Put the lid on the potjie, bring to the boil and cook for 2½ hours until the samp is soft. Control the heat by adding or removing flames and coals, so it's not boiling rapidly but you've got slightly more heat than a very gentle simmer. Let's call it a medium-paced simmer. If at any stage it looks like it's too dry in there, add a little more water. The water level inside the potjie should be just about visible from the top between the samp and beans.
7. When you think the samp is pretty much soft, add the onion soup powder and stir it in gently until it is well mixed. Continue to simmer the meal uncovered for another 15 minutes until most of the moisture has evaporated and you have a thick meal ready to be enjoyed off the plate, and not just from a soup bowl. If this is not the case yet, continue to cook uncovered until it is!
8. Taste the umngqusho – if you like it more salty, add a bit of salt. The stock and onion soup powder already added salt to the meal, so taste first.
9. Take it off the fire and stir in the cheese. Your work of African art is now ready to serve.

PERI-PERI SAUCE

This sauce can be used and served with absolutely everything at your braai. Bread, vegetables, rice, pap and whatever else you think needs a kick. Due to the combination of ingredients, it will easily last for weeks in your fridge and the flavour gets even better after standing for a few days. I suggest you make it in large quantities.

WHAT YOU NEED
(feeds 8–10)

FOR A JAR YOU CAN KEEP
IN YOUR FRIDGE
(feeds 10, but if your sauce is
very hot, it might feed more)

8 garlic cloves (crushed and chopped)

½ cup olive oil

½ cup grape vinegar
(red or white)

½ cup lemon juice

½ cup water

1 tot paprika

1 tot chilli powder

1 tot salt

a few small hot chillies
(peri-peri/African bird's eye, chopped)

FOR ONCE-OFF USE
(sometimes you don't need
a whole jar of peri-peri; if so,
use these quantities)

2 garlic cloves (crushed and chopped)

1 tot olive oil

1 tot grape vinegar

1 tot lemon juice

1 tot water

1 tsp paprika

1 tsp chilli powder

1 tsp salt

1 or more small hot chillies
(peri-peri/African bird's eye, chopped)

WHAT TO DO

1. Finely chop the garlic and throw this into a glass bottle or jar (with at least 500 ml capacity), along with the oil, vinegar, lemon juice, water, paprika, chilli powder and salt. Shake well until the ingredients are mixed and all the salt dissolved.
2. Now taste the sauce and if you want it hotter, add a few finely chopped chillies to the sauce and shake. You can add as many chillies as you wish but remember that you can never expect your guests to eat a sauce that is too hot for them. If, like me, you like quite a lot of burn then it might be wise to mix two batches – one with fewer chillies.
3. Do not touch your eyes or any other sensitive parts of your body while you are making this sauce as the traces of chilli juice left on your hands will burn those sensitive parts. Go and wash your hands to get the chilli juices off them, and then still be careful.
4. The sauce can be used immediately but will improve with age and last in your fridge for weeks.

AND ...

The use of peri-peri chillies and sauces filtered into South Africa from our Portuguese-speaking neighbouring countries Mozambique and Angola. The peri-peri (also called African bird's eye or piri-piri) chilli is a member of the Capsicum family of chillies. Compared to the average chilli, it's quite small and very hot. If you can't get hold of it, use any small and potent chilli. But the best is to get yourself a plant and cultivate them at home; they grow quite easily in most parts of South Africa.

NAMIBIAN CHIMICHURRI SAUCE

No, it's not from South Africa but it is from Argentina via Namibia – two countries also known for open-fire cooking (what we call braai)! During a braai excursion to our neighbouring country, Namibia, we spent a night at Op My Stoep Lodge in Oranjemund. The owner, Fanie, is originally from Argentina and gave me his chimichurri sauce recipe after my very nice meal. According to him, this sauce gets better with a day or two in the fridge for the flavours to marry properly, and this is true. But truth be told, I have never waited that long.

WHAT YOU NEED
(feeds 4)

4 long red chillies (seeded and chopped)

4 long green chillies (seeded and chopped)

2 garlic cloves (crushed and chopped)

½ tot dried oregano

½ tot coarse salt

1 tsp ground black pepper

1 tot white wine vinegar

2 tots olive oil

½ cup flat-leaf parsley

WHAT TO DO

1. Mix all the ingredients for the sauce together and place in a food processor or blender. Blend until everything is smooth and has a good, even consistency.
2. In theory, you should put the sauce in a closed container and let it rest in a fridge for at least 2 days. In reality, you might consume it on the same day.
3. Serve the sauce with bread, vegetables like potatoes or sweet potatoes, or anything else at your braai.

JAN BRAAI PIZZA

This will probably become one of your favourite go-to recipes. It's so simple you might one day even question why it was in a recipe book at all. Whether you are craving it, want to impress guests, or are on a road trip and want to do a quick scenic and hassle-free braai, this is a nice trick to have up your sleeve.

I first made this on the *Jan Braai vir Erfenis* television show a few years ago and it went cult overnight. In those first few weeks of the Jan Braai Pizza, many supermarkets sold out of ready-made pizzas on a daily basis, such was the demand. The possibilities with toppings are endless and you can use whatever your favourite off-the-shelf pizzas are. I usually go for two store-bought pizzas with different toppings and then manually add some extra feta cheese before going to the fire. Enjoy!

WHAT YOU NEED
(feeds 2–4)

2 store-bought pizzas (raw but prepared, with the toppings of your choice)

something extra (including but not limited to feta cheese, garlic, mushrooms, capers, olives, roasted vegetables or sundried tomatoes)

a hinged grid

WHAT TO DO

1. Light a fire and wait till the coals are the same heat that you would braai your braaibroodjies on – in other words, medium heat.
2. Place the two pizzas on top of each other with the fillings facing to the inside. If you want to add anything extra, do so beforehand.
3. Place the pizza sandwich in your hinged grid, close the grid tightly, and braai the pizza, turning it often, the same as you would do with a braaibroodjie. You want the outside to be toasted and crispy and the cheese on the inside to be completely melted.
4. Once you have achieved the perfect pizza, take it off the grid, slide it onto a wooden board and cut into slices. Serve immediately.

CHEESE FONDUE

There is obviously no need to buy expensive fondue equipment in order to enjoy a traditional cheese fondue. Just make the sauce in one of your smaller cast-iron potjies over the fire. Once the sauce is ready, move the potjie away from the fire and place a few coals under it to keep the cheese sauce warm and runny, and then tuck in.

WHAT YOU NEED
(feeds 4 as a main meal)

1 block Brie cheese (about 125 g)

1 block Camembert cheese (about 125 g)

1 block Cheddar cheese (about 150 g)

1 block Gruyère cheese (about 150 g)

½ tot cornflour (Maizena)

1 clove garlic (peeled, but whole)

1 cup white wine

1 tot brandy

cumin powder (optional)

1 large loaf of bread, cut into bite-sized chunks (get something nice like a sourdough bread, or at least a baguette)

WHAT TO DO

1. Remove the rinds from all the cheeses. Chop the soft cheeses (Brie and Camembert) into cubes, and grate the hard cheeses. Sprinkle the cornflour over the cheese and toss around. You want the cheese to be thinly dusted with the cornflour.
2. Rub the inside of your small to medium-sized cast-iron potjie with the piece of garlic.
3. Now put the potjie over coals or a few flames. Pour all of the wine into the pot and bring to a simmer.
4. Add all of the cheese to the simmering wine. Keep stirring while the cheese melts.
5. As soon as you have a smooth sauce, stir in the tot of brandy. Take the potjie off the fire and keep the sauce warm while you enjoy dipping in.
6. If you like cumin, sprinkle a bit of ground cumin into the potjie. I like cumin; hence, I often do this – but it's optional.
7. Serve with chunks of bread, which everybody can dip into the sauce with suitable implements like sosatie sticks and braai forks.

AND ...

You can also dip boiled baby potatoes, cooked butternut, cherry tomatoes or mini gherkins into the sauce. The traditional Swiss cheese fondue recipe calls for the use of a cherry liqueur known as Kirsch. But this is South Africa and we're preparing the fondue on a fire, so obviously you should rather use brandy. I've had fondue in Switzerland a few times and my South African version tastes better.

BRAAI AUBERGINE PITA

Depending on whether you prefer speaking Greek, Turkish or Arabic around the braai fire, you might also like to call this meal a gyro, döner or shawarma – it's really up to you. Whatever language you speak, the important thing is to gather around a fire. Everyone loves this meal and, as a bonus, it looks great in photos.

WHAT YOU NEED
(feeds 6)

6 pita breads
2 large aubergines

FOR THE MARINADE
1 tsp coriander seeds
1 tsp cumin seeds
1 tsp salt
1 tsp ground black pepper
2 garlic cloves (chopped)
1 lemon (juice)
3 tots olive oil

FOR THE YOGHURT SAUCE
1 cup double-cream yoghurt
½ cucumber (chopped)
1 tot olive oil
2 garlic cloves
(finely chopped)

FOR THE SALAD
2 big tomatoes (or 12 cherry tomatoes, chopped)
½ cucumber (the other half)
1 smallish red onion (or half a big one, finely chopped)
1 tot fresh mint
1 tot fresh parsley
1 tot fresh oregano
1 tot olive oil

WHAT TO DO

1. Crush the coriander and cumin seeds in a pestle and mortar, and mix in the salt, pepper, garlic cloves, lemon juice and olive oil. Make the marinade by combining all the ingredients.
2. Cut the aubergines into 1cm-thick slices and use all the marinade to baste the slices of aubergines.
3. Prepare the yoghurt sauce by combining all ingredients in a bowl and mixing well.
4. Make the salad by chopping and combining the tomatoes, cucumber, onion, mint, parsley and oregano. Add a bit of olive oil to give it that nice shine.
5. Braai the aubergine slices over hot coals, turning a few times until done. They should be completely soft and a bit charred on the sides.
6. As the aubergines come off the fire, immediately add the pita breads to the grid and toast them for a few minutes, turning a few times and taking care not to let them burn.
7. Open the toasted pita breads and evenly distribute the various ingredients into them, starting with the salad, then the aubergines, and ending with the yoghurt sauce.

BRAAIED CAMEMBERT

Compared with some of my other favourite cheeses, Camembert has a fairly low melting point. The outside skin has a much higher melting point than the inside though. This makes it the perfect cheese to braai as is. No need to put it in bread, in a pan or in foil – just take it out of the packaging and braai over medium to low coals for about 10 minutes until the cheese on the inside has melted, but before the outside skin melts, boils or ruptures. There are plenty of ways to serve braaied Camembert and my favourite is like this, with nuts and figs as a dessert. This way the coals of your fire are nice and relaxed post-dinner by the time you want to braai the cheese.

WHAT YOU NEED
(feeds 4)

4 whole rounds Camembert cheeses (about 125 g each)

about 20 pecan nut halves (shelled)

8 ripe figs (or preserved if you can't find fresh ripe ones)

WHAT TO DO

1. Braai the Camembert cheeses on an open grid (I don't like the pressure a closed hinged grid puts on them). You don't want the coals to be too hot as you want the insides to melt before the outsides burn or break. Turn them about 3 times during the braai using either your recently washed hands or a clean pair of braai tongs. If you're using tongs to turn them, take care not to press too hard and damage the cheese.
2. During the braai also toast the nuts in a dry pan for about 1 minute, just until they start to get colour but before they burn.
3. You will be able to feel when the cheese is ready (when it goes soft on the inside). Remove from the fire, plate and then cross-cut them open like you would do with a jacket potato.
4. Open the top of the braaied skin and serve with figs and toasted nuts.

AND ...

As a starter, you can braai the Camembert cheeses in exactly the same way, open them up and serve with a spoon of berry jam.

NACHOS POTJIE

Many of the recipes in this book are ones I have been doing for years; many have been published in one of my other books before. They just happen to exclude meat and hence, they are proudly re-published here. But not this recipe.

During the process of writing this book, I also looked at innovative new things to do on the braai that do not involve meat. One of the best things I did was develop this particular recipe. It was an instant hit and at the time of publishing this book, is one of my all-time favourites. For me, it ticks all the boxes: Widely available ingredients. Easy process (from starting to eating takes well under an hour). Looks great. Tastes amazing.

WHAT YOU NEED
(feeds 4)

FOR THE TOMATO RELISH
1 tot olive oil

1 onion (chopped)

2 bell peppers (green, yellow or red, chopped)

3 garlic cloves (crushed and chopped)

1 tot paprika

½ tsp chilli powder

1 tsp cumin

1 tsp ground coriander

1 tsp mixed dried herbs

1 tin chopped tomatoes

1 tin red kidney beans

¼ beer (roughly 80 ml, drink the rest)

salt and pepper (to taste)

300 g Cheddar cheese (grated)

TO SERVE
1 pack tortilla chips (I use normal triangle-shaped tortilla corn chips, such as Doritos)

2 mielies

2 avocados (out of the skin and chopped into blocks)

sour cream

fresh coriander

WHAT TO DO

1. Place your potjie on the fire and heat the oil, add the onion and peppers, and cook until soft. Add the garlic, paprika, chilli powder, cumin, ground coriander and dried herbs, and cook for another minute.
2. Add the tomatoes, beans and beer and let this simmer with the lid on for about 15 minutes. Remove the lid and continue to simmer so that the sauce can reduce until it is thick. Regularly stir and scrape along the bottom of the potjie to ensure the sauce doesn't burn.
3. Add the grated cheese, place the lid on the potjie and let this melt for a few minutes.
4. While you are preparing the relish in the potjie, also braai the mielies on a grid over hot coals, turning them often and letting the kernels char a bit. Time step 3 and 4 to be finished at the same time. When the mielies are done, after about 15 minutes, remove from the fire and then use a sharp knife to cut off all the kernels. Mielies straight off the fire are quite hot so hold them with gloves or tongs.
5. Serve the meal by using a big spoon to scrape the tomato relish to one side of the potjie and then placing the chips in the space that you formed. Now artfully add the avocado, sour cream and mielies, and then garnish with fresh coriander.

BABY POTATOES WITH GARLIC, BUTTER AND ROSEMARY

This is my original baby potato recipe, and the foundation for the two other recipes that follow. These baby potatoes are right in line with the character of this book – they're very easy to make, yet look impressive and taste great! I boil them first, and then fry them with whole cloves of garlic in butter and rosemary. You squash the potatoes to burst them slightly while they are frying so that the butter and the other flavours can be properly absorbed. It's all done in one pot too, so there's a minimum of dirty dishes.

WHAT YOU NEED
(feeds 6 as a side dish)

1 kg baby potatoes (washed)
125 g (¼ of a 500 g brick) **butter** (diced)
1 tot olive oil
a sprig or 3 of rosemary
all the cloves of one head of garlic (peeled and whole)
1 tsp salt
1 tsp black pepper

WHAT TO DO

1. Boil the potatoes in salted water for about 15 minutes until they are tender (test with a knife or fork).
2. Take the pot off the heat and drain the potatoes. Now put the pot back on the fire and add the butter, olive oil, rosemary, garlic, salt and pepper to the potatoes.
3. Stir until all the butter has melted, and heat further until the butter starts to fry the potatoes. Using a potato masher, the back of a wooden spoon or the bottom of a wine bottle, press down lightly on each potato until they crack open ever so slightly and start to absorb the flavoured butter. Cook for about 10–15 minutes until the potatoes and garlic are golden brown and crispy. You can gently toss or turn the potatoes, but you don't want them to fall apart as we're not making mash here.
4. I like to serve this meal straight from the pot, as the cast iron holds its heat and keeps the potatoes warm until they are on everyone's plates.

AND ...

I have a bit of a love–hate relationship with rosemary. It goes very well with some meals, like this one, and you absolutely need to add it. However, in my eating experience some people frequently destroy meals by adding too much rosemary, which then dominates the meal in an unpleasant way. I can only speculate, but think that this is because rosemary is the one herb that grows easily and successfully in most gardens across South Africa. Amateur botanists who fail to nurture most things, find that their rosemary plant flourishes. These people are so proud of the one success story in their herb gardens that they want to show off with it at every opportunity they get, and so go a bit overboard when adding rosemary to food.

PAPRIKA AND CHEESE POTATOES

This is quite obviously great. Potatoes cooked soft in a potjie and then cast-iron-potjie-fried in olive oil and butter. Add to that star players like paprika – the fresh version, also known as sweet bell pepper; paprika – the dried, ground version; and cheese. It is what winning feels and tastes like.

WHAT YOU NEED
(feeds 6)

1 kg baby potatoes

2 tots olive oil

2 tots butter

1 onion (chopped)

1 bell pepper (green, yellow or red, seeded and sliced into strips)

8 garlic cloves (crushed)

1 tsp salt

1 tsp pepper

300 g Cheddar cheese (grated)

½ tot paprika

WHAT TO DO

1. Wash the potatoes, add them to your potjie and boil in water until soft.
2. Now drain the water from the potjie but keep the soft-boiled potatoes in the potjie. Add the olive oil, butter, chopped onion, bell pepper strips, garlic, salt and pepper to the potjie and now stir-fry everything for a few minutes until some things become caramelised and golden brown.
3. Now use your wooden spoon or braai tongs and press on some of the potatoes so they burst at the seams, allowing some extra flavours to develop and penetrate the potatoes. Stir-fry for another minute or 3.
4. If things at the bottom of the potjie get sticky and want to burn, add a bit of water, olive oil, beer, wine or stock and scrape loose anything sticky.
5. You now add the grated cheese and sprinkle paprika on top of that. Close the lid of the potjie and take the potjie off the fire. Add a generous helping of coals onto the lid of the potjie – as much as you can fit onto the lid – and wait a few minutes for the cheese to start melting. Once the cheese has melted, your potatoes are good to go!

THE ULTIMATE POTATO POTJIE

This very fancy baby potato recipe has one step that I find keeps the guest who wants to help busy – and that is, removing the olive pits. So whichever guest first asks how they can help, ask them to do this. After they've washed their hands, of course. Apart from that, your effort-to-impress ratio is very good here, and you've done your good deed for the day – because everyone will be very impressed with the meal and now the guest who helped you can also claim a bit of credit for helping.

WHAT YOU NEED
(feeds 6 as a side dish)

1 kg baby potatoes (washed)

3 tots butter

1 tot olive oil

1 onion (chopped)

8 garlic cloves
(peeled but whole)

250 g button mushrooms

a sprig or 3 of rosemary

1 tsp salt

1 tsp black pepper

1 cup pitted black olives

1 packet (250 g) **sundried tomatoes in oil** (drained and chopped)

1 tot fresh parsley (chopped, to serve)

WHAT TO DO

1. Put your potjie on the fire and cook the potatoes in salted water for about 20 minutes until they are tender (test with a knife or fork).
2. Take the pot off the fire and drain the potatoes. Now put the pot back on the fire and add the butter, olive oil, onion, garlic, mushrooms, rosemary, salt and pepper to the potatoes.
3. Stir until all the butter has melted, and heat further until the potatoes start to fry in the butter. Using a potato masher, the back of a wooden spoon or the bottom of a wine bottle, press down lightly on each potato until they crack open ever so slightly and start to absorb the flavoured butter, oil and other juices.
4. Cook for about 10–15 minutes, using a wooden spoon to ensure everything gets browned but nothing burns. Continue until the potatoes, mushrooms, onions and garlic are golden brown. You can gently toss or turn the potatoes, but you don't want them to fall apart as we're not making mash here.
5. Now gently stir in the olives and sun-dried tomatoes and continue to fry the whole lot for a few minutes.
6. I like to serve this meal straight from the pot, as the cast-iron holds its heat and keeps the potatoes warm until they are on everyone's plates. Sprinkle with the chopped parsley and serve. If you want to go even bigger here, add some crumbled feta cheese to the potjie, topping it all off just before serving.

CURRIES

JAN BRAAI VEGETARIAN CURRY

My signature vegetarian curry potjie. Enjoy!

WHAT YOU NEED
(feeds 6)

2 tots olive oil

1 onion (chopped)

2 garlic cloves (crushed and chopped)

1 cup lentils

2 tots medium curry powder

1 tot ground coriander

1 tot ground cumin

1 tot paprika

1 tsp turmeric

about 400 g butternut (peeled and chopped)

about 300 g sweet potato (peeled and chopped)

1 tin chopped tomatoes

1 sachet (50 g) **tomato paste**

400 ml tin coconut milk

1 cup vegetable stock

1 tin chickpeas (drained and rinsed)

1 tin kidney beans (drained and rinsed)

salt and pepper (to taste)

fresh coriander (to serve)

sour cream or double-cream yoghurt (to serve)

WHAT TO DO

1. Heat the oil in your potjie on the fire and fry the onion until translucent.
2. Now add the garlic, lentils and all the spices. Fry for another minute or 2 but proceed to the next step before the spices burn. If you are losing control and things get overly sticky and want to burn, just add a bit of water to regain control.
3. Now add the butternut and sweet potato and toss with everything else already in the potjie.
4. Next you add the tomatoes, tomato paste, coconut milk and stock. Stir everything until mixed and place the lid on the pot.
5. Now let it simmer for 15 minutes and then add the chickpeas and kidney beans. Mix and put the lid back on.
6. Simmer over medium heat for at least 30 minutes until all the vegetables are soft and cooked through. During this time you can occasionally lift the lid to slide your wooden spoon along the bottom of the potjie and gently toss everything. You don't want anything to break apart but you also don't want anything to stick to the bottom of the potjie and burn.
7. If at any stage you feel that the potjie is running dry and wants to burn, add a bit more water. This should not be the case though.
8. Taste the potjie and season with salt and pepper.
9. Serve with fresh coriander and sour cream or double-cream yoghurt.

SIDE DISHES FOR CURRY

TOMATO AND ONION SALAD

WHAT YOU NEED
(feeds 8)

4 tomatoes (chopped)
1 red onion (finely chopped)
2 tots fresh coriander (chopped)
2 tots fresh mint leaves (chopped)
1 red chilli (chopped)
1 tot olive oil
1 lemon (juice)
salt and pepper

WHAT TO DO
Mix all the ingredients together, season with salt and pepper, and serve fresh with your curry.

CUCUMBER AND YOGHURT

WHAT YOU NEED
(feeds 8)

1 cucumber (chopped or grated coarsely)
2 cups Greek yoghurt (or full-cream yoghurt)
1 tot mint (freshly chopped)
1 tot parsley (freshly chopped)
salt and pepper
1 tsp paprika

WHAT TO DO
Mix the first four ingredients together, season with salt, pepper and paprika, and serve fresh with your curry.

BANANA AND COCONUT SALAD

WHAT YOU NEED
(feeds 4–6)

1 cup fine dry coconut
3 bananas (sliced)
1 lemon (juice)

WHAT TO DO
1. Dry-roast the coconut in a pan until it just starts to brown.
2. Place the bananas in a bowl and drizzle with the lemon juice. Sprinkle the coconut over the bananas, and serve with your curry. Make this sambal just before you eat it, not days in advance.

HOW TO COOK BASMATI RICE

WHAT YOU NEED
(feeds 4–6)

6 cups boiling water
½ tot salt
1 cup basmati rice

WHAT TO DO
1. In a large pot on the fire or stove, bring the water and salt to the boil.
2. While you wait for the water to boil, place the rice in a strainer or sieve and rinse properly under cold running water for about a minute, making sure most of the starch is rinsed away.
3. Once the water is boiling, add the washed rice to it and cook for 12 minutes.
4. Drain the rice in a strainer or sieve and quickly rinse with hot water. Let it drip dry, and then decant the rice into a bowl.
5. Leave it to stand for a bit and separate the grains with a fork if necessary.

BAKED BEANS BUNNY CHOW

Culinary-wise, and I don't mean this in a negative way, the bunny chow is probably the single biggest contribution Durban has made to South African society. As any South African worth their braai salt knows, the bunny chow is essentially curry served in a hollowed-out piece of bread loaf. If you like your curry as hot as Upington in the middle of summer, add the optional chilli powder. If you want it mild, use less chilli powder or skip it altogether and trust the masala to provide the necessary kick.

WHAT YOU NEED
(makes 4 quarter-loaf bunnies)

2 tots olive oil

2 onions (sliced or chopped)

3 garlic cloves (crushed and chopped)

fresh ginger, equal in volume to the garlic (finely chopped or grated)

1 tot masala (curry powder, your choice of mild, medium or hot)

1 tsp chilli powder (optional, for the extra-hot bunny)

2 tins baked beans

2 potatoes (cut into small cubes)

2 carrots (cut into slices)

1 cup water

1 tsp salt

½ tsp black pepper

1 loaf fresh white bread (you need absolutely stock-standard normal white bread, and you need it unsliced so that it can be cut to specification)

1 punnet fresh coriander (to serve)

WHAT TO DO

1. Heat the oil in a potjie over a medium-hot fire and fry the onion for about 5 minutes until it becomes soft.

2. Then add the garlic, ginger, masala and (optional) chilli powder, and fry for 1 minute until the pan becomes sticky. If at any stage during step 1 or 2 you have too much heat in the potjie and things start to burn (in a charred way, not a chilli way), add a very little bit of water as a counter-attack – but only do this if it's really necessary. We need the flavour to develop by means of getting a bit sticky at the bottom of the potjie.

3. Throw in the baked beans, potatoes, carrots, water, salt and pepper, then stir, scraping the bottom of the potjie with your spoon to loosen any and all sticky bits.

4. Cover with a lid and simmer over medium-low coals for about 30 minutes, stirring now and again so that the bottom of the potjie doesn't burn. If no amount of stirring is going to stop the dish from burning, it means your potjie is too dry. Add a bit of water to rectify this but go easy. You're making curry, not soup.

5. Continue to simmer until the potatoes are soft. Check whether they're cooked through by sticking a fork or knife into them. As soon as the potatoes are soft, the meal is essentially ready. Cook uncovered for a few minutes to allow the sauce to become a thick gravy and then the curry is done, so take the potjie off the fire. Taste and adjust with a bit of extra salt if it needs it.

6. Cut the loaf of bread into quarters and then scoop or cut out the centres of each quarter loaf, essentially creating a 'bowl' of bread for the curry. You're basically creating four bowls made of bread. Fill the hole of each quarter loaf with the curry and sauce. Serve the scooped-out bread centre and fresh coriander leaves on the side.

AND ...

The stock-standard, non-sliced white bread is increasingly becoming somewhat of an endangered species in upmarket supermarkets. If you're from the side of town that only sells sliced bread, I would skip that and rather serve each person their curry in whatever is the most substantial but basic white bread roll you can find.

GREEN CURRY

A basic Thai curry sauce should be quite versatile – almost like your favourite pair of braai tongs. The key ingredient is the green curry paste, and this is available at most supermarkets. Not all curry pastes are equal in strength, so if some of your friends or family members are sensitive to the odd bit of chilli in food, rather err on the side of caution when using a new green curry paste until you know what degree of ferocity you're dealing with.

WHAT YOU NEED
(feeds 4)

1 tot vegetable oil

1 tot green curry paste

3 garlic cloves (crushed and chopped)

fresh ginger, equal in volume to the garlic (chopped or grated)

1 green chilli (finely chopped, optional)

1 tin (400 ml) **coconut cream or coconut milk**

1 packet (usually around 375–400 g) **mixed seasonal vegetables** (containing things like baby marrows, carrots, broccoli, cauliflower and green beans)

½ tot lemon juice (or lime juice)

salt (to taste)

½ cup fresh coriander (chopped)

roosterkoek, roti or basmati rice (to serve)

WHAT TO DO

1. Heat the oil in a potjie on a medium-hot fire. Add the curry paste, garlic and ginger, and fry for about 1 minute until you can smell how good it's going to taste. Watch it so that it doesn't burn, which can happen quite quickly. If you know that you and your guests like it hot, this is the time to add one or more chopped green chillies. I'm not the type of person who removes the seeds from chillies. After all, the point of adding the chillies is to add some fire to the meal. However, if you are the type of person who drinks caffeine-free coffee with fat-free milk, by all means remove the seeds.

2. Now add the coconut milk and heat it up until there is a simmer. If anything started sticking to the bottom of the pot in step 1, use your spoon to negotiate it loose from the bottom and mix it with the rest of the sauce.

3. Add the vegetables and cook them in the sauce for about 10 minutes. You want a medium level of boiling in the pot, so it's more than a simmer but less than a rapid boil. Your vegetables must still be al dente and crunchy at the end. Add the lemon juice and stir well. Taste and add salt if it's needed.

4. Take the potjie off the fire and stir in the chopped coriander leaves. Serve with warm roosterkoek, roti (page 130) or rice, and garnish with a few extra coriander leaves.

BUTTERNUT BUTTER BEAN BUTTER CURRY

Butter curry is arguably the most popular of all Indian curries. Lovers of spicy food universally enjoy it and this potjie suits a wide range of palates. I've met very few people in my life who don't enjoy this dish, so if you're nervously scanning through this book looking for a sure-fire winner before braaing for a tough crowd of in-laws, this is it.

WHAT YOU NEED
(feeds 4)

125 g (½ cup or ¼ of a big block) **butter**

1 tot vegetable oil

1 onion (finely chopped)

2 garlic cloves (crushed and chopped)

fresh ginger, equal in volume to the garlic (chopped or grated)

1 tsp red chilli powder

1 tsp turmeric

1 tsp coriander

1 tsp cumin

1 tsp fennel seeds (or 1 tsp ground fennel/barishap)

4 cardamom pods

4 cloves

100 g cashew nuts (crush the nuts in your pestle and mortar)

1 tin tomato purée (these are normal-sized tins of about 410 g – don't confuse with tomato paste, which is the thicker one in smaller cans, nor with chopped tomatoes)

1 tin evaporated milk

500 g butternut (peeled and cut into small blocks)

1 tin butter beans (drained)

1 tsp salt

½ tsp black pepper

roosterkoek, roti or basmati rice (to serve)

fresh coriander (roughly chopped, optional, to garnish)

WHAT TO DO

1. Add the butter, oil and onion to your potjie and put it over a medium-hot fire. When the butter has melted, let the onion fry for a few minutes until it starts to soften but not brown. It might look like a lot of butter, but this is butter curry after all.

2. Throw in the garlic, ginger, chilli, turmeric, coriander, cumin, fennel, cardamom, cloves and cashew nuts, then fry for another minute or 2 until stuff gets sticky and looks like it wants to burn. Before it burns, immediately proceed to the next step.

3. Pour in the tomato purée and evaporated milk, then bring to the boil and stir everything well. Use your wooden spoon to scrape all over the bottom of the potjie and ensure nothing is sticking to it.

4. Add the butternut and drained tin of butter beans, and season with the salt and pepper. Stir everything through and put the lid on the potjie. Let it simmer for 45 minutes until the butternut is completely soft. Lift the lid every so often to toss the contents of the potjie gently and to ensure there is enough liquid and it's not burning. If things get dry, add a dash of water.

5. When the butternut is soft and you like the look and consistency of the sauce, remove the potjie from the fire. Serve with roosterkoek, roti (page 130) or basmati rice and garnish with chopped coriander.

THE BEAN ROGAN JOSH

This is a superb curry with a rich and exotic flavour. Amazingly, all the spices you need are available at normal South African supermarkets and the red kidney beans and cannellini beans are equally widely available. Each ingredient serves a purpose in creating the aromatic end product. Take a deep breath and just follow the steps – this is one of the easier yet more impressive potjies you will make in your life.

WHAT YOU NEED
(feeds 4)

2 tots vegetable oil

2 onions (peeled and finely chopped)

2 bay leaves

1 cinnamon stick

6 green cardamom pods

6 whole black peppercorns

6 whole cloves (the spice, not garlic)

6 garlic cloves (crushed and chopped)

fresh ginger, equal in volume to the garlic (crushed or chopped)

1 tsp ground coriander

1 tsp ground cumin

1 tot paprika

1 tsp cayenne pepper

1 tsp salt

1 tin red kidney beans (drained)

1 tin cannellini beans (drained)

1 cup double-cream yoghurt

½ cup water

roosterkoek, roti or basmati rice (to serve)

fresh coriander (to garnish)

WHAT TO DO

1. Heat the oil in a potjie on the fire. Fry the onions for about 5 minutes until they start to soften. Add the bay leaves, cinnamon stick, cardamom pods, peppercorns and cloves, and fry for about 1 minute. Right about now you will smell some great things happening in the pot as the heat starts to release fragrances from the spices.

2. Add the garlic and ginger, and stir-fry for another minute, then add the coriander, cumin, paprika, cayenne pepper and salt. Stir these in well. The mixture might be fairly dry at this point, which means things could burn, so don't have big flames under the pot. It also means you should move along quickly to the next step.

3. Add the two tins of drained beans and mix it all together. If your potjie is looking a bit dry and the spices are sticking to the bottom, add a small bit of water to help with this.

4. Add the yoghurt while stirring continuously to mix it well into the dish.

5. Cook for 2 minutes, then add the water, and stir until you have a sauce as smooth as the Protea cricket players. Bring to the boil, then cover with a lid and gently simmer over low heat for about 30 minutes until the sauce has reduced to form a rich gravy. If your fire is too hot, the gravy will reduce too quickly and become a burnt paste, which would be a tragedy. Watch the heat carefully and stir a few more drops of water into the pot if really necessary.

6. Take the pot off the fire and serve with roosterkoek, roti (page 130) or basmati rice and some fresh coriander leaves.

AND ...

Cardamom pods are like referees in rugby matches. Without them, the meal cannot exist, but they are not particularly pleasant things to encounter. They are at their best if you don't actually notice that they're there. If you spot one in the finished product, pick it out and throw it away. It has already served its purpose of adding flavour to the meal.

SWEET POTATO KORMA

Korma is one of the world's most popular curries and is traditionally prepared in a potjie on the fire. It's been around since way before the days of electricity, and back then this was really the only way to do it. Prepare it with the actual spices, as opposed to using a pre-mixed masala or paste. Even though it is spicy, the korma is relatively mild and quite creamy, so it suits a wide variety of palates. And you're unlikely to need to down jugs of water and milk after enjoying it.

WHAT YOU NEED
(feeds 4)

1 tot olive oil

1 tot butter

2 onions (chopped)

500 g carrots (peeled and sliced)

4 garlic cloves (crushed and chopped)

fresh ginger, equal in volume to the garlic (grated)

1 tsp ground coriander

1 tsp cayenne pepper (or chilli powder)

1 tsp cumin

5 cloves (whole)

5 cardamom pods

1 cinnamon stick

2 tots tomato paste (or a 50 g sachet)

500 g sweet potatoes (peeled and in blocks)

1 tin coconut cream or coconut milk

100 g ground almonds

salt and pepper (to taste)

roosterkoek, roti or basmati rice (to serve)

fresh coriander (to serve)

WHAT TO DO

1. Add the oil and butter to your potjie on the fire. Add the chopped onion to the potjie and fry the onion for a few minutes until it gets some colour.
2. Now add the carrots and stir-fry for another few minutes.
3. Then add all the other condiments and spices, and toss around for about 1 minute until it has the type of fragrance that makes your neighbours jealous. The potjie could get quite dry and run the risk of burning in this step, so add a splash of water if needed.
4. Add the tomato paste, stir everything through and then add the sweet potatoes.
5. At this stage, there might be some sticky bits on the bottom of the pot, trying to burn themselves onto the pot and take up permanent residency there. Add a dash of water to the potjie, and use a wooden spoon to scrape and negotiate it all loose.
6. Now stir in the coconut cream and then close the lid of the potjie. You want it to simmer for the next 30 minutes with the lid closed.
7. After 30 minutes, stir in the ground almonds. Don't close the lid again – just let the potjie simmer uncovered until the carrots and sweet potatoes are soft, you like the consistency of the sauce and you are ready to eat.
8. As with absolutely every potjie you ever make on a fire, when you are almost entirely but not quite happy with the consistency, taste the potjie and add salt and pepper to taste if needed.
9. Serve with roosterkoek, roti (page 130) or basmati rice, as well as fresh coriander and any other curry side dishes of your choice (page 118).

RAINBOW NATION ROTI

Roti is a type of bread which, as you know, also goes by the name chapati, but in South Africa we generally refer to it as the former. The purpose of a roti is similar to a wrap or pancake, that is, you use it to carry some other food to your mouth. When it comes to curry, roti is often the vehicle of choice. In Cape Town where I live, a meal of curry wrapped in roti is referred to as a salomi. Rotis are very easy to make and go well with all the curry potjie recipes in this book.

WHAT YOU NEED
(makes 8)

2 cups normal white flour
(plus some extra flour for kneading)

1 tsp salt

½ cup water

butter (for spreading)

WHAT TO DO

1. Shake, throw or sift the 2 cups of flour and the salt into a bowl. Add a little bit of water at a time, and keep stirring with your wooden spoon. Once all the water is in, start kneading the dough on a floured surface until it is soft and stretchy. The longer you knead it, the softer your rotis will be.
2. Now divide the dough into 8 equal-sized balls.
3. Use a wine bottle or something similar to roll out the individual balls on a floured surface until they are about the size of your whole hand (about 15 cm) in diameter and very thin. Add more flour to both sides while rolling to make the process easier.
4. Heat your fireproof pan and cook each roti for about 20 to 30 seconds in a dry, very hot pan until bubbles start to form on the roti's surface. Turn it over and cook on the other side for an equal amount of time. They are done when they are slightly puffed up, start to brown, and there are dark spots here and there. Cook each roti individually this way.
5. Now you need to keep the rotis warm until you are ready to eat them. Use a bowl or plate that you can put on a cooler spot on your grid. Place a kitchen towel in the bowl. As you finish cooking each roti, spread butter on it and fold into a quarter of its whole size by folding the circle in half and then in half again, with the buttered side on the inside. Wrap it up inside the towel. Keep piling the buttered, folded rotis inside the kitchen towel until you are done with all of them. They are best served hot and fresh so don't prepare them the day before.
6. Serve with one of the great curry potjies from this book.

SOUP

BRAAIED BUTTERNUT SOUP

It's a fact: braaied butternut soup tastes better than ordinary butternut soup. It gets extra flavour when you braai the butternut and onions over the coals. I reckon the main reason all top restaurants don't prepare their butternut soup this way is because they don't have braai facilities in their kitchens.

Once cooked, all you need to transform the contents of the potjie into soup is a potato masher. When you're at home it's easier to use a stick blender though, which also makes the soup smoother.

WHAT YOU NEED
(feeds 6–8)

1.5 kg butternut
(you might need 2, 3 or 4
butternuts, depending on size)

1 large onion

1 litre vegetable stock

½ tsp dried thyme
(or 1 tsp fresh chopped thyme)

½ tsp salt

½ tsp black pepper

1 cup cream (250 ml tub)

**fresh bread with butter for
serving** (optional)

WHAT TO DO

1. Peel the butternuts and slice into 2 cm-thick slices. Use a spoon to scrape out the pips and other innards growing in the cavity. Slice the onion in half without peeling it.
2. Braai the butternut and onion on an open or hinged grid over hot coals for about 5–10 minutes. Your aim at this stage is not to cook them completely; you just want the surface a bit charred.
3. When ready, put the braaied butternut and onion in a bowl. Now take off and throw away the outer layer and ends of the onion as you would with any other onion you are about to chop, and then chop the onion.
4. Prepare the stock by boiling the water in your potjie or kettle on the braai or in the kitchen. Add the stock powder or blocks as per the instructions on the packaging. If you're feeling confident, do steps 2 and 4 at the same time.
5. Add the braaied butternut, braaied and chopped onion and thyme to the stock in the potjie and bring to the boil. Put the lid on the pot and cook for 15–30 minutes until the butternut is completely soft and starts to fall apart. You can take the lid off now and again to check that the soup is boiling but not burning, and to check when the butternut is completely soft.
6. Remove the potjie from the fire. Use a regular potato masher (or electric stick blender) and transform the contents of the potjie to soup. Season with salt and pepper.
7. Add the cream and stir well – the texture should be thick but not too solid. If yours is too thick, just add a bit of extra water until you're happy with the consistency.
8. Put the potjie back near the fire to keep the soup hot until you want to serve it.

AND ...

You get bonus points if you serve the soup with freshly braaied roosterkoek.

MINESTRONE

This one is pretty straightforward as far as soup goes as you leave minestrone in its natural chunky form. You just have to put your potjie over a fire and then add the ingredients as described in each step. Every region (and almost every household) in Italy has its own version, and there is no standard recipe for minestrone. There is no definitive ingredient either, but the inclusion of cannellini beans is very traditional and that's why I use them in my recipe. If you've never had the confidence to make potjiekos before, start off with this recipe.

WHAT YOU NEED
(feeds 8)

2 tots olive oil

1 onion (finely chopped)

2 celery stalks
(finely chopped)

2 carrots (peeled and
finely chopped)

2 garlic cloves (crushed
and chopped)

6 cups (1.5 litres) **water**

2 cups vegetable stock

1 tin cannellini beans
(drained)

2 tins chopped tomatoes

1 cup pasta (uncooked,
small shapes)

1 cup shelled peas (I use
frozen peas)

salt and pepper (to taste)

Parmesan cheese (grated,
to serve)

fresh bread (optional,
to serve)

WHAT TO DO

1. In a large potjie (no. 3) over a medium-hot fire, heat the oil and then throw in the onion, celery and carrots. Fry for about 10 minutes until the vegetables start to soften. Add the garlic at the end and fry for 2 minutes.
2. Add the water, stock, beans and tomatoes to the pot. Cover with a lid and bring to a simmer. Cook for 15 minutes.
3. Take off the lid and add the pasta. Simmer for a further 10 minutes or until the pasta is soft but not soggy.
4. Add the peas and stir well. The frozen peas will be ready to eat by the time you dish up.
5. Taste the soup and season with salt and pepper according to your own taste. The stock already contains salt, so it's possible that the soup may not need extra salt.
6. Serve in deep bowls with grated Parmesan cheese and bread.

CURRIED SWEET POTATO AND CARROT SOUP

A potjie and a fire do a great job when it comes to cooking soup. The special piece of equipment I have to make this recipe particularly successful is a cordless stick blender. Once all the contents of the potjie are cooked, you use the blender to transform the lumps into a smooth soup right there on the fire. Alternatively, just use a traditional potato masher for a soup with a slightly different texture but equally great taste.

WHAT YOU NEED
(feeds 8)

2 tots olive oil

1 onion (chopped)

3 garlic cloves (chopped)

fresh ginger, equal in volume to the garlic (grated or chopped)

2 tsp medium curry powder

1 tsp ground coriander

1 tsp cumin

2 medium-sized sweet potatoes (peeled and cut into blocks)

4 large carrots (peeled and cut into chunks)

2 cups good-quality vegetable stock

1 cup water

1 lemon (juice)

1 tot fresh coriander (chopped)

salt and pepper (to taste)

1 tub sour cream (or crème fraîche)

fresh bread (optional, to serve)

WHAT TO DO

1. Heat the oil in a potjie on the fire and fry the onion for 4 minutes. Add the garlic and ginger, and fry for another minute.
2. Add all the spices and fry for about 1 minute until it starts smelling amazing.
3. Now stir in the sweet potato and carrot, making sure everything is mixed well with the spices.
4. Add the stock and water. Bring to a gentle boil and close the lid of the potjie. Simmer for about 45 minutes until everything is cooked and completely soft. You can check up on the potjie now and then just to make sure it's not running dry, but this is very unlikely. As usual, if this does happen, add more water.
5. Once everything is cooked through and soft, remove the lid and use your stick blender or masher to transform the contents of the potjie into a soup of uniform consistency. If the soup is too thick, add some water.
6. Stir in the lemon juice and coriander. Taste and season with salt and pepper.
7. Dish up with a big dollop of sour cream or crème fraîche in each bowl and serve with fresh bread toasted on the fire.

BRAAIED TOMATO SOUP

As is, tomatoes are pretty healthy. Full of vitamins and rich in antioxidants. They contain natural sugars and exposing those to the searing heat of a wood fire releases a whole pan full of flavours. Roasting them over a fire for a soup naturally imparts some additional smoky aromas into the meal as well, and you are creating a tomato soup vastly superior to anything that a fancy restaurant can offer. This recipe can stand on its own as a light main meal but obviously also does the trick as the first course in an expansive multi-course braai showcase. The correct way to serve braaied tomato soup is with a cheese braaibroodjie.

WHAT YOU NEED
(feeds 6)

FOR THE SOUP
2 tots olive oil

2 red onions (chopped)

4 garlic cloves (peeled and crushed)

1 kg tomatoes (a combination of different types of tomatoes, halved or quartered)

1 tsp salt

1 tsp pepper

1 tot balsamic vinegar

1 cup white wine

1 cup vegetable stock

few sprigs of fresh herbs (like basil, oregano and parsley)

stick blender

1 cup fresh cream

FOR THE CHEESE BRAAIBROODJIES
12 slices white bread

butter (to spread on bread)

200 g Cheddar cheese (grated)

200 g mozzarella cheese (grated)

WHAT TO DO

1. Place the olive oil, onion, garlic and tomatoes in your potjie and season with the salt and pepper. Place the pot onto the fire on very high heat and let the tomatoes start to cook.
2. As soon as the ingredients start to stick to the bottom of the potjie, add the balsamic vinegar, toss everything around with your wooden spoon and let that get even more sticky.
3. Before anything burns, add the white wine and stock. Use the liquid to scrape loose anything that is stuck to the bottom of the potjie.
4. Now let the soup simmer for 15 minutes with the lid on the potjie and then remove it from the heat.
5. Add your selection of fresh herbs, and then use your stick blender to transform the contents of the potjie into a smooth soup.
6. Stir in the cream and now let the soup simmer for another 10 minutes to generate extra flavour in the vicinity of the fire.
7. During this time of the soup casually sitting close to the fire, you can taste it and season with extra salt, pepper and a little bit of sugar if you feel any of those are needed.
8. Proceed to make and braai the cheese braaibroodjies and as soon as they are ready, the soup can be served.

WHAT TO DO FOR CHEESE BRAAIBROODJIES

1. Spread butter on one side of each slice of bread (this will be the outside of your braaibroodjie). With the buttered sides facing outwards, evenly distribute the grated cheese onto six slices of bread and close with the other six slices of bread.
2. Place the braaibroodjies in a closed hinged grid and braai over medium-hot coals.
3. Remember, a braaibroodjie is a draaibroodjie, so turn often until all the cheese is melted and the outsides are golden brown.

MIELIEPAP
& BREAD

PUTU PAP IN A POTJIE

There are but three principles to successfully making putu pap (also known as krummelpap). They are:
1. managing the water:maize meal ratio,
2. building an iceberg, and
3. using a two-tined fork.

WHAT YOU NEED
(feeds 5–6)

2 cups water
1 tsp salt
3 cups maize meal

WHAT TO DO

1. Bring the water to the boil and add the salt.
2. Remove the pot from the flames.
3. Pour all the maize meal into the water, aiming for the centre of the pot. You should now have an 'iceberg' of maize meal in the pot, with the lower part under water and the top part sticking out of the water in the centre.
4. Put the lid on and place a few coals under the pot. You want a slight bubble from the water every now and again, but essentially the rest of the water now needs to steam into the maize meal.
5. You can check once or twice that there is enough heat and that steam is in fact being generated, but don't check too often as steam will escape every time you lift the lid, and that steam is supposed to go into the maize meal, not into the clear blue sky.
6. After 20 minutes remove the lid and use the two-tined fork to break the iceberg. Vigorously stir all the porridge and any leftover water drifting around in the pot until the contents look like putu pap.
7. If you think it all looks a bit dry, add some water (cold or hot) and stir it in with the two-tined fork.
8. Replace the lid and let it continue to steam on gentle heat for another 20 minutes.

AND ...

As you can see, this recipe is very easy. For more putu pap, increase your ingredients but stick to the same ratio. It's quite common for the maize meal to form a crust at the bottom of the pot. Do not worry about this. Simply treat the top of this crust as the new 'bottom' of your pot. After the whole process is finished and all the porridge has been eaten, this crust can be removed quite easily. You can even heat the pot just before removing the crust and then eat the crust with a bit of butter.

MIELIEPAP WITH SWEETCORN

The single greatest drawback of living in Cape Town is that mieliepap is not the staple food at every braai. Fortunately I get to braai all over South Africa often and so never have to go without it for too long. My fellow South Africans, wherever you live in this beautiful country of ours, we need to eat more mieliepap. It works well with a breakfast braai, lunch braai and dinner braai. It goes well with absolutely any braaied food. Cook less rice and more mieliepap!

WHAT YOU NEED
(feeds 4–6)

4 cups water

2 cups maize meal

1 tsp salt

1 tin creamed sweetcorn

1 tot butter

WHAT TO DO

1. Put the water, maize meal and salt in your potjie. Bring to the boil over a hot fire while stirring.
2. Reduce the heat to a light simmer, cover with the lid and cook for 20 minutes, occasionally lifting the lid to stir. If at any time you feel things are a bit dry and might burn, just stir in a bit more water.
3. The total simmer time for pap is about 30 minutes. After about 20 minutes, add the sweetcorn and butter, give it a good stir and replace the lid for the last 10 minutes of cooking.
4. The pap should now be ready to serve but if not, let it simmer a bit longer, stirring in more water if necessary.

CHAKALAKA

Chakalaka is pretty straightforward to make, and very tasty to eat. There are thousands, if not millions of recipes in South Africa. When calling for submissions for my crowd-sourced book *Shisanyama*, I received many options, so when developing this recipe, I looked for the common threads of golden truth running through all the different versions. This, then, is a triple-distilled version. A best of the best, if you will.

WHAT YOU NEED
(feeds 6)

3 tots olive oil

3 onions (chopped)

3 garlic cloves (crushed and chopped)

1 tsp fresh ginger (grated)

2 fresh chillies (chopped)

3 bell peppers (any combination of green, yellow or red, seeded and chopped)

4 carrots (peeled and grated or chopped)

2 bay leaves

1 tot medium curry powder

1 tot paprika

1 tin chopped tomatoes

1 sachet (50 g) **tomato paste**

1 tin baked beans

salt and pepper (to taste)

fresh coriander (to serve)

WHAT TO DO

1. Heat the oil in your potjie and fry the onion until translucent.
2. Next, add the garlic, ginger, chilli, peppers, carrots and bay leaves, and just toss with the onions.
3. Now add the curry powder and paprika, then fry for another minute to toast the spices but proceed to the next step before things burn.
4. Add the chopped tomatoes and tomato paste and mix well. Put the lid on the potjie and leave to simmer over medium to low heat for 30 minutes so the flavours can develop and the carrots and anything else that's hard can cook soft.
5. Add the beans, mix through and simmer for another 10 minutes.
6. Taste and season with salt and pepper if you feel the need.
7. Serve with fresh coriander, paired with putu pap (page 144).

MIELIEPAPTERT

In a world of uncertainty, I have never been disappointed by mieliepaptert. It's an almost foolproof dish. You start off by making mieliepap – already a great meal on its own. Then you just add some bells and whistles to make it even better – almost like buying a great new car and then adding all the optional extras. Most recipes will tell you to assemble the mieliepaptert in layers and I used to do that. But emancipate yourself from this slavery: you can simply mix it all together for ease of preparation and an even better marrying of flavours. Why struggle when things can be easy?

WHAT YOU NEED
(feeds 8)

FOR THE STYWEPAP
2 cups maize meal

3 cups water

1 tsp salt

FOR THE MIELIEPAPTERT
2 tots olive oil

1 onion (finely chopped)

400–500 g mushrooms
(sliced)

½ tsp salt

½ tsp black pepper

1 tin creamed sweetcorn

2 cups cream

2 cups (about 200 g) **Cheddar cheese** (grated)

1 tin chopped tomatoes

2 sprigs fresh thyme
(optional, to garnish)

WHAT TO DO FOR THE STYWEPAP

1. Stir the maize meal and water together in a pot to mix well. Add the salt, stir and close the lid.
2. Let it simmer on low heat, lifting the lid occasionally to stir, for about 30 minutes until cooked.
3. Remove the pot from the fire and remove all the pap from the pot. Set the pap aside for later use.

WHAT TO DO FOR THE MIELIEPAPTERT

1. Put the pot back on the fire. Add the oil, onion and mushrooms. Fry for about 10 minutes until the onion turns a golden-brown colour. Season with salt and pepper.
2. Now add your cooked pap, break it up into big chunky pieces and mix everything together in the potjie.
3. Add the sweetcorn, cream and grated cheese and stir well. Lastly add the tin of tomatoes and stir that in. We want streaks of red through the white.
4. Close the lid. Add coals on top of the lid and let the potjie bake over medium heat for 30 minutes. We don't want it burning so if you feel that might happen before the 30 minutes are up, remove from the fire immediately.
5. Once done, remove from the fire and let it rest for about 10 minutes before serving so that the whole meal can thicken. Garnish with fresh thyme.

ROOSTERKOEK

Baking bread is an ancient skill, and a fulfilling one, so you need to master it. The tricky part is making the dough. If you've never made dough in your life, the recipe below will probably look quite daunting the first time you read it. Take a deep breath, drink a beer, and read it again. Like riding a bicycle, it's surprisingly easy once you get the hang of it.

WHAT YOU NEED
(makes 12 decent-sized roosterkoek)

1 kg cake flour (as the 'koek' part of the Afrikaans name implies, use cake flour – but white bread flour is also fine if that is what's on hand)

10 g instant yeast (it comes in 10 g packets)

1 tot sugar

½ tot salt

lukewarm water in a jug (you'll need roughly just more than 2 cups of water)

2 tots olive oil

WHAT TO DO

1. Sift the flour into a bowl that is at least 3 times as big as 1 kg of flour, and preferably even bigger. If you're in the middle of the bush and don't have a sieve on hand, then skip the sifting part and just chuck the flour into a big enough bowl. If you only have a 1 kg bag of flour and no more, save a little for step 9.
2. Add the yeast and sugar to the flour and mix thoroughly with your clean hand. Now it's time to add the salt and toss the mixture around some more.
3. Pour in the lukewarm water bit by bit and keep kneading the dough. As soon as there is no dry flour left, you've added enough water. Take care not to add too much water, as this will lead to the dough being runny and falling through the grid. Roosterkoek falling through the grid is just no good. For 1 kg of flour you'll probably use just a tiny bit more than 2 cups of water.
4. If you think you have enough water in there, add the 2 tots of olive oil.
5. Knead the dough well for about 10 minutes until none of it sticks to your fingers anymore and it forms one big pliable piece.
6. Cover the bowl with a kitchen towel and put in a warm area for 10 minutes.
7. Take off the kitchen towel and knead the dough again for 1 or 2 minutes.
8. Replace the kitchen towel and let it rise for at least 30 minutes.
9. Use your recently washed hands to flatten the dough onto a table or plank that is covered in flour and also lightly sprinkle flour on top of the dough. Your aim is to create a rectangular or square piece of dough.
10. Use a sharp knife and cut the dough into squares, and let them rise for a few minutes one final time.
11. Bake over very gentle coals for about 15–20 minutes, turning often. A roosterkoek is ready when it sounds hollow when you tap on it. Alternatively, insert the blade of your pocketknife or multi-tool into them as a test. If the blade comes out clean the roosterkoek is ready.

AND ...

Some supermarkets sell fresh dough. If you've bought some of that, start making your roosterkoek from step 9.

If you've never made dough in your life, there's no shame in asking someone who has done it before to show you what it means to 'knead it into one pliable piece'.

POT BREAD

Making the dough for pot bread is slightly easier than making the dough for roosterkoek as it's not such an issue if you add a little bit too much water. The bread is baked in a pot and the dough is going nowhere, unlike a runny roosterkoek that will sink through the grid. Baking bread in a pot comes at a price though as you cannot see what is going on, so burning the bread is a greater risk.

WHAT YOU NEED
(feeds roughly 12)

1 kg white bread flour (or cake flour if that is what's on hand)

10 g instant yeast (instant yeast comes in 10 g packets, specifically done that way to make it easy, as you need 10 g for every 1 kg of flour)

1 tot sugar

½ tot salt

lukewarm water in a jug (you'll need roughly just more than 2 cups of water)

2 tots olive oil

butter (for serving)

WHAT TO DO

1. Sift the flour into a bowl that is at least 3 times bigger than 1 kg of flour, but preferably even bigger. If you are in the middle of the bush and do not have a sieve on hand then skip the sifting part and just chuck the flour into a big enough bowl.
2. Add the yeast and sugar to the flour (do not add the salt yet) and mix thoroughly with clean hands.
3. Add the salt and toss around. (Adding salt directly onto yeast will kill the yeast.)
4. Add the lukewarm water bit by bit and knead the dough continuously. When there is no dry flour left, you've added enough water. For 1 kg of flour you will probably use about 2½ cups of water.
5. Once you have enough water in there, add the 2 tots of olive oil.
6. Knead the dough properly for about 10 minutes until none of it sticks to your fingers anymore and it forms one big pliable piece. If this simply never happens, you added too much water. Add more flour to fix it.
7. Cover the bowl with a damp kitchen towel or cling wrap and place in a warm area for 10 minutes. During this time you need to smear the inside of the pot and bottom of the lid really well with butter.
8. Remove the kitchen towel or cling wrap and knead the dough again for a minute or 2. Now put the dough into the pot. There needs to be space for the bread to rise when the lid is on. If there isn't enough space, the pot is too small. Remove some of the dough and bake roosterkoek with it.
9. Place the pot in a warm area and let the bread rise in the pot for 30 minutes.
10. Now you need to bake the pot bread in even heat for about 1 hour. Even heat means all parts of the pot, and bread, need to be equally exposed to the heat. If there is a very hot fire nearby you need to turn the pot regularly. Place the pot on coals and also place coals on the lid. As the coals below or on top of the pot start to cool off, replace them with new ones. Never add too much heat, or it will burn. I usually take it quite easy on the heat when baking pot bread for fear of burning the thing but it's entirely possible your bread will be ready in 40 minutes; you will have to check.
11. A pot bread is ready when it sounds hollow when you tap on it (you'll need to remove the lid to do this). Then insert the blade of a pocketknife into it as the final test. If the blade comes out clean the pot bread is ready. Sometimes you burn a pot bread. It's just one of those unfortunate facts of life. If you don't, give yourself a pat on the back. If you do, just cut away the burnt part and adjust your technique slightly next time.

GARLIC BREAD

What an extraordinary meal. Works very well as a snack around the fire and fits equally well as a side dish to any braaied food. There's a reason why homemade garlic bread tastes better than the ones you buy in the supermarket: when you make your own garlic bread, you use a fresh baguette that you bought that day. When you buy ready-made garlic bread at the store, who knows how stale that bread might be?

WHAT YOU NEED
(feeds 4–6)

1 baguette (French loaf)
½ cup salted butter (soft)
5 cloves garlic (crushed or chopped)
1 tot fresh parsley (chopped)
½ tot lemon juice
1 tsp pepper
a roll of tinfoil
Cheddar cheese (or Parmesan, optional)
chilli (chopped, optional)

WHAT TO DO

1. If the baguette is very long, make two shorter garlic breads.
2. Slice the baguette into 2 cm-thick slices, but keep those slices in order. Your ability to keep those slices in the right order is one of the distinguishing factors between good and awesome garlic bread.
3. Heat the butter slightly so that it's nice and soft. Now mix the butter, garlic, parsley, lemon juice and pepper together.
4. Keeping the bread slices in order, place them on a piece of tinfoil that is large enough to wrap the whole bread in. Always place the bread on the foil before you butter it. Any butter you spill will be wrapped up in the foil and be absorbed by the bread.
5. Spread the butter onto one side of each slice and place it back on the foil in order. Make sure the butter goes right to the edges of each slice. On the finished product, another distinguishing factor in garlic bread quality is whether the edges of each slice are dry or whether they were properly buttered.
6. If there is any leftover butter, spread it over the top of the bread.
7. Wrap the garlic bread tightly in foil and braai for 12 minutes over high heat, turning to expose all sides to the heat. As the bread is tightly wrapped in foil and will not absorb all that much flavour from the braai, you may also prefer to bake it in an oven on 180 °C for 12 minutes.

AND ...

If you want to make the garlic bread business class, also mix 1 cup grated Cheddar into the butter. If you want to make it first class, mix grated Parmesan cheese into the butter. If you want to make it a fighter plane, mix in a chopped chilli with your choice of cheese.

STOKBROOD

As you've noticed by now, I don't think braaing has to be limited to things on grids. We can also do it in potjies and pans or, as in this case, on a stick. Braaing stokbrood is a great family activity. When I was young we used to do it all the time while camping in the Cederberg. Not only does it keep your kids busy, but it also introduces them to some basic principles of braaing: using gentle heat and turning often so that the inside is done before the outside burns. My favourite fillings for stokbrood are butter (never ever margarine) and golden syrup (for some reason, I prefer it to honey on a stokbrood), or grated Cheddar cheese and apricot jam.

WHAT YOU NEED
(makes 8–10)

1 kg cake flour

10 g instant yeast
(1 small packet)

1 tot sugar

½ tot salt

2 tots olive oil

about 2½ cups water
(slightly warm)

washed wooden sticks
(the thickness of a broomstick)

WHAT TO DO

1. Throw the flour, yeast, sugar and salt into a very large mixing bowl and mix well with one of your recently washed hands.

2. Add the oil and just more than 2 cups of water (I usually need about 550–600 ml) and mix well with your hands to form a soft dough. Start with 2 cups, and then add a little more water if the mixture is too dry. Continue to mix until the dough comes together as a ball.

3. Move this dough ball to a clean, flat surface (wooden board, table top, kitchen counter, bonnet of your bakkie) and knead for about 5 minutes until the dough is smooth, elastic and in one pliable piece. Don't add any extra flour unless the dough is really very sticky – you'll see the texture usually changes quite rapidly from sticky to elastic while you're kneading it.

4. Put the dough back in the mixing bowl and cover it with a damp kitchen towel or plastic wrap. Let it rise for about 30 minutes until double in volume.

5. When ready, turn the dough out onto a lightly floured surface (wooden board, table top, kitchen counter, bonnet of your bakkie), then knead for a few strokes, just to punch out some of the air (as the Springbok front row does when scrumming against the Australians).

6. Divide the dough into 8–10 pieces and then roll out each piece into a long strip of around 30–40 cm.

7. Start at the one end of a stick and attach the end of a piece of dough onto it. Press it slightly so that it can't come loose too easily. Now roll the dough around the stick from the top, until you get to the end of the piece of dough. Tuck in the end to make sure it doesn't come loose. (If you don't have enough sticks, just do this and the next part in batches.)

8. You can now proceed to braai the stokbrood or you can leave the rolled coils of dough on the sticks in an upright position for a few minutes to rise again. Over medium-hot coals and turning often, braai the stokbrood for about 15 minutes until it has a nice brown shine. If your arms get tired, there are all sorts of creative ways involving kids or rocks to make your stokbrood stand on its own.

9. When the stokbrood comes away from the stick easily, it is ready.

AND ...

You can buy new pieces of wood for your stokbrood at most hardware stores. Ask for the wood to be cut into 1-metre-long pieces, a safe length that will ensure all braaiers leave with their eyebrows intact. Alternatively just consult the nearest tree regarding some dead branches.

POT-ROASTED BUNS

We all agree on the cult status of braaibroodjies, or as the Queen refers to them, South African fire-toasted braai sandwiches. But there are also two other major players in the braai-bread market. They are, of course, roosterkoek – bread rolls baked on the grid – and potbrood, which is a bread baked in your potjie on the fire. What follows below drew inspiration from various recipes, most heavily from a recipe sent to me by Leana. And so, for our next magic trick, we're packing the flavour right into the dough and we're giving the rolls the brilliant benefit of some potjie taste!

WHAT YOU NEED
(feeds 8)

olive oil (for frying)

1 onion (chopped)

500 g white bread or cake flour

1 packet (10 g) **instant yeast**

1 tot sugar

½ tot salt

1 cup Cheddar cheese (grated)

1 tot fresh oregano (chopped)

1 cup water (lukewarm)

2 tots olive oil

1 cup cream

butter (to serve)

WHAT TO DO

1. Heat some oil in your fireproof pan and fry the chopped onion until soft. You can also do this step on the stove in your kitchen.
2. Place the flour, yeast, sugar and salt into a mixing bowl, and mix until well combined. Add the onion, cheese and oregano, and mix well.
3. Add a little bit of lukewarm water to the mixture and mix well, adding a bit more water at a time until you have what resembles a dough. You will need roughly 1 cup of lukewarm water for 500 g of flour, but add a little more if you need to.
4. Use clean hands to knead the dough on a floured surface for a few minutes until it is soft and elastic.
5. Place the dough mixture back into your mixing bowl, and leave it in a warm place; for example, the general vicinity of the fire or covered with a cloth in the sun. Leave it to rise for about 30 minutes.
6. After half an hour, knock down the dough, kneading for another few minutes.
7. Add olive oil to your no. 10 flat-bottomed potjie, making sure the bottom and all the sides are coated in oil.
8. Shape the dough into balls, somewhere between the size of golf balls and tennis balls, and pack them into the potjie in a single layer.
9. Pour the cream over the dough balls and sprinkle any extra grated cheese you coincidently have lying around over that.
10. Now put the lid on the potjie and bake over medium coals, also adding a few coals to the top of the potjie lid. Don't be overly aggressive – bread has a tendency to burn.
11. After about 40 minutes, carefully lift the lid, making sure that no ash or coal from the lid falls into the potjie. The bread should be golden brown and baked. Serve warm from the fire, lathered with butter.

CORNBREAD

There is a man by the name of Russell, who is responsible for a lot of the behind-the-scenes work on my books – after I write them and all the photos are taken, up until they end up on the shelves of bookstores. This recipe is a collaborative effort between that man and myself, and is born from our shared love of cornbread baked at the fire.

WHAT YOU NEED
(feeds 10)

1 tot olive oil or butter
(to grease the potjie)

2 cups white bread or cake flour

2 cups maize meal

1 tot baking powder

½ tot salt

1 fresh mielie (slice the kernels off the cob)

1 tin (400 g) **creamed corn**

2 eggs

1 cup milk

1 tot olive oil (part of the batter)

more butter (to serve)

WHAT TO DO

1. Use olive oil or butter to grease the inside of your no. 10 flat-bottomed potjie properly.
2. To this greased potjie, add all the dry ingredients and mix together well.
3. Now add the wet ingredients and mix properly again. Don't overmix. As soon as everything is mixed, that is sufficient.
4. Put the lid on the potjie and gently bake this bread for about 1 hour. Have the potjie on a stand or grid with some coals under it, and also put some coals on the lid of the potjie. Periodically, add extra hot coals below and on top.
5. Although your aim is 1 hour, some fires are hotter than others so after about 45 minutes, you can check, as it might be done. Insert a sharp knife into the bread and if the knife comes out clean, the bread is ready. If not, check in another 15 minutes.
6. Now you have two options. The better option is to break pieces or chunks of bread from the potjie, lather them with butter and enjoy. If, however, you are from the conservative side of the culinary spectrum and think all bread needs to be served in neat slices, then allow the bread to cool down a bit before turning it out, as it can be quite difficult to remove the bread from the potjie straight off the fire – and very fresh, hot bread is difficult to slice. It can take up to 45 minutes to cool, and by that time, all the cool kids will have eaten the bread straight from the potjie.

AND ...

Salted butter is better than unsalted butter. It's just the way it is. Never, ever, under any circumstances, serve this bread with margarine as margarine is evil. Eating this bread with margarine will lead to 7 years of bad luck followed by another 7 years of even worse luck.

ORIGINAL SOUTH AFRICAN BEER BREAD

The beer bread, in its simplest form, has two ingredients: a classic bottle or can of beer and a 500 g packet of self-raising flour. By my reckoning and experience you can't go wrong when you add a tot of olive oil and a teaspoon of salt to this mix. This brings you to 4 basic ingredients and you have a bread. But 5 is such a nice round number that you might as well add one more thing to get your bread to that magic 5-wicket haul.

WHAT YOU NEED
(feeds 4–8)

additional olive oil or butter
(to coat the inside of the potjie)

500 g self-raising flour

1 tsp salt

2 wheels feta cheese (150 g, drained and crumbled)

1 tot olive oil

1 normal-sized normal beer
(330–340 ml)

WHAT TO DO

1. Use olive oil or butter and rub the inside of your no. 10 flat-bottomed baking potjie with a coating of your chosen non-stick agent.
2. To this potjie, add the flour, salt and feta cheese. Mix this with one of your recently washed hands.
3. Now add the olive oil and beer. Using one of your recently washed hands or a wooden spoon, mix and knead all the ingredients until they are combined. Do not work too hard here and over-exert yourself. As soon as everything is properly combined you're good to proceed to the next step. If your beer happened to be a bit bigger than usual and you are worried that the mixture is too 'wet', don't worry about it, just carry on. If you sneaked a few sips of the beer before adding it to the bowl and your mixture is too dry, add a bit of water or milk.
4. Place the lid on the potjie and bake for around 45 minutes with coals underneath the pot and on top of the pot's lid until the bread is done. You will know when it's ready by looking at it, tapping on it and then inserting a knife to see whether it comes out clean.
5. Take care not to burn the bread; there is no risk whatsoever in baking it a bit slower and taking an hour, for example.

AND …

There is no limit to the number and variety of additional ingredients that you can use in your beer bread. Always add the 4 core ingredients but the feta cheese can be swapped with a cup of grated Cheddar cheese, chopped and fried onion, a tin of sweetcorn, a tin of chakalaka, sundried tomatoes, fresh herbs … the list goes on!

SUPER SODA BREAD

When I say super, I mean super easy and when I say soda, I mean we use baking soda (bicarbonate of soda) as the raising agent. Let me explain. From an effort point of view, there are three types of bread: flatbread, bread made with yeast, and bread made with baking soda.

Flatbread types use no raising agent whatsoever and are consequently flat, like a roti. Then there is yeasted bread that uses some form of yeast to make it rise. To activate, this yeast takes time and you need to knead the dough. Our third bread category uses baking soda to create bubbles in the dough to make it rise.

Unlike yeast, baking soda does not need to be kneaded to do its work. In fact, many expert bakers agree that when using baking soda, not only should you knead the dough as little as possible, you should actually not knead it at all! I know what you're thinking and yes, this is super fantastic news. The baking soda needs something to react with and we will use buttermilk for that something, as it will also add some taste to the bread. Although you can quite successfully bake a lily-white soda bread, I prefer the taste and coarse texture of wholewheat and oats. When you're travelling the backroads and get hold of a truly great jar of jam at a farm stall or market, this is the bread it deserves.

WHAT YOU NEED
(feeds 6–8)

butter (for oiling the potjie)

3 cups Nutty Wheat flour (or wholewheat flour)

1 cup oats

1 tsp baking soda

1 tsp salt

1 bottle buttermilk (2 cups)

WHAT TO DO

1. Smear the inside of your no. 10 flat-bottomed baking potjie generously with butter.
2. Put all the ingredients, except for the buttermilk, into a mixing bowl and mix well.
3. Now add the buttermilk and stir with a wooden spoon until everything is combined. Remember, not only is it unnecessary to knead the dough, it is better not to. So as soon as everything is properly mixed you are good to go.
4. Flop the dough into the prepared potjie, dust the top of the bread with some extra flour (this is purely for cosmetic purposes) and use your favourite and sharpest pocketknife to cut a cross in the top of the bread. As with the flour dusting, this cross is only for cosmetic purposes and makes no real contribution to the taste of the end product. (But we all know good-looking food tastes better.)
5. Now close the lid and bake for about 45 minutes until done. You want some coals under the potjie and some coals on the lid. When any particular coal loses motivation, discard it and replace with a new one. There is no particular risk in baking the bread too slowly but if you rush it, it might burn so rather err on the side of caution.
6. After 45 minutes, remove the lid, taking care not to spill too much ash onto the bread. A bit of ash is fine, again, for cosmetic purposes. Insert the tip of a knife into the bread and if it comes out clean, the bread is ready.
7. If the bread does not stick to the potjie at all and comes out whole, great. If it sticks to the bottom of the potjie a bit, don't worry. Take a spatula, go in on the lines of the cross you cut earlier and take it out in quarters.

AND...

This recipe works with any combination of 4 cups of flour. You could drop the oats and go with just 4 cups of Nutty Wheat or wholewheat flour. Or use 2 cups of Nutty Wheat and 2 cups of normal white flour. You get my drift.

DESSERT

MOSBOLLETJIES WITH BRAAIED BANANA BUTTER

Jan Hendrik van der Westhuizen is one of South Africa's top export products. He is a great chef, world class to be exact, and he took traditional South African-style recipes to the fancy people in France. His food is in fact so awesome that they gave him a Michelin star which, unlike those in the sky, doesn't come along every day. Jan Hendrik was kind enough to share his legendary mosbolletjie recipe with me for publication. It's served with braaied banana butter, because everything tastes better off the fire.

WHAT YOU NEED

FOR THE DOUGH
1 kg white bread or cake flour
½ cup sugar
20 g (2 packets) **instant yeast**
1 tot aniseed
½ tot salt
1 cup grape juice
1 cup water
½ cup milk
250 g (half a big block) **salted butter**

FOR THE BUTTER
4 bananas
250 g (the other half of the big block) **salted butter** (at normal braai-area temperature)

WHAT TO DO

1. Add the flour, sugar, yeast, aniseed and salt to a mixing bowl and mix well.
2. Heat the grape juice, water, milk and butter together in a pot or pan and stir. It does not need to boil – it just needs to be warm. Like water when you shower.
3. Now add the warm liquid to the dry ingredients and mix everything through.
4. Wash your hands and then start to knead your dough for about 10 minutes until the dough is looking sexy. I say 10 minutes because Jan Hendrik says 10 minutes, but in real life, I usually get tired after 5 minutes and proceed to the next step. But Jan Hendrik has a Michelin star and an army of sous chefs at his disposal to do the hard yards so obviously 10 is better but 5 is fine.
5. Cover the dough with a damp kitchen towel and let it relax for 30 minutes.
6. After 30 minutes, the dough should have risen. Now knead the dough again for 5 minutes. This second round of kneading is a signature aspect of mosbolletjies. You can skip it but then you're cheating.
7. Once done, roll small balls of dough, somewhere between the size of golf balls and tennis balls, with your hands. Pack these mosbolletjies nice and firm next to each other in your well-buttered no. 10 potjie.
8. Put the lid on the potjie and let the mosbolletjies rise for about 20 minutes in a safe, pleasant and warm spot next to your fire.
9. Once they have doubled in size, gently bake on medium-hot coals for 50–60 minutes. You want the potjie on a stand, with some coals under it. Also place a few coals on the lid to make sure it gets enough heat from all sides. Your mosbolletjies are ready when you insert a skewer or knife into the middle and it comes out clean.
10. During the time that you are baking the mosbolletjies, aggressively braai the bananas, skin and all, on the fire until the bananas turn black and they start oozing with caramel texture. Remove from the fire and allow them to cool down a bit. Then scoop out the banana flesh into a bowl. Mix the braaied caramelised banana flesh with soft butter and using your wooden spoon until everything is combined. Keep this butter in a fridge until the mosbolletjies are ready.
11. Serve your mosbolletjies with a generous helping of banana butter.

CHOCOLATE FONDANT POTJIE PUDDING

There is a medical reason why you should eat chocolate. The scent of the chocolate increases theta brain waves, which induces relaxation. We all know how vitally important it is to destress, relax and feel good about your life. And this is why you and your loved ones should consume the baked chocolate potjie as often as possible. It will make you a better person.

WHAT YOU NEED
(feeds 8)

FOR THE BATTER
1 egg
3 tots butter (melted)
½ cup milk
½ tot vanilla essence
1 cup self-raising flour
1 tot cocoa powder
pinch of salt
½ cup sugar
2 small slabs dark chocolate
(80 g each, broken into
blocks)

FOR THE SAUCE
1½ cups brown sugar
2 tots cocoa powder
1½ cups boiling water

TO SERVE
fresh cream or ice cream

WHAT TO DO

1. **Make the batter, part 1:** In your no. 10 flat-bottomed baking potjie, whisk the egg and then use your wooden spoon and mix the butter, milk and vanilla with the whisked egg.

2. **Make the batter, part 2:** Now mix the flour, cocoa, salt, sugar and chopped chocolate pieces into the wet mixture of step 1. Just use the sugar and cocoa specified as ingredients for the batter, not the sugar and cocoa for the sauce, which only comes in the next step. Everything needs to be mixed properly so use a wooden spoon and put in some effort. If you're unfit get one of your friends or family members to help you, or buy yourself a cordless stick blender (it changed my life).

3. **Make the sauce:** Stir the sugar, cocoa powder and boiling water together until all the sugar has dissolved and the mixture is smooth. Slowly pour this hot cocoa-sugar-water mixture over the dough mixture that is already in the pot.

4. **Bake:** Put the lid on the potjie and bake for 25 minutes by placing coals under the pot and a lot of coals on the lid of the pot. Your work of art is ready when the top is firm to the touch.

5. **Serve:** with fresh cream or ice cream.

RED WINE PEARS

Fresh fruit is always welcome around the braai fire. Especially when it's sweet, flavourful, comes with a red wine sauce and is served as dessert. Make sure you use firm pears for playing this game as they will hold their shape better after cooking in the red wine. Always use the quality of wine you would also drink. If you were supposed to use something that tastes like vinegar, the name of the recipe would have been 'Vinegar pears' but it isn't. Once done, you can also serve these pears with soft mascarpone cheese or ice cream instead of the blue cheese and pecan nuts, but then it is not going to look this cool on photos.

WHAT YOU NEED
(feeds 6)

6 pears (firm but ripe)

1 packet pecan nuts (100 g, chopped roughly)

1 bottle good red wine

2 tots soft brown sugar

1 thick strip of orange peel

juice of that same orange

1 cinnamon stick

2 cloves (actual cloves, not garlic cloves)

1 star anise

1 block blue cheese (200 g, crumbled)

WHAT TO DO

1. Peel the pears with a vegetable peeler, leaving the stalk still in place. The stalk makes absolutely no difference to how they taste but it does make them look cool.
2. Get your potjie on flames and dry-toast the pecan nuts for about 2 minutes until they start to smell like they want to be part of the meal but before they burn. Immediately remove them from the potjie before they do exactly that, and burn.
3. Place the wine, sugar, orange peel and juice, and all the spices into your now empty potjie, stir to mix, and bring the mixture to the boil.
4. Add the pears, put the lid on the potjie and let it simmer for 40 minutes until the pears are soft. Turn the pears often, making sure they colour evenly all over. Once the pears are soft but still firm, remove from the potjie and set aside. It's fine if they cool down partially or completely.
5. Bring the sauce to the boil again and reduce until it becomes more like a syrup. During this time, taste the sauce and if you want it sweeter, add a bit more brown sugar to it.
6. Serve the pears with crumbled blue cheese and a sprinkling of pecan nuts, and top it off with the wine reduction from the potjie.

BRAAIED BANANA AND CARAMELISED PINEAPPLE

Braaied banana and caramelised pineapple with ice cream and golden syrup is every bit as good as it looks on paper.

WHAT YOU NEED
(feeds 6)

1 pineapple

sugar (brown or white)

6 bananas

ice cream (or cream or crème fraîche)

golden syrup

WHAT TO DO

1. Peel the pineapple and cut into six slices of even thickness. Coat both sides of each pineapple slice in sugar by either dipping it in sugar or sprinkling sugar over both sides. The bananas are braaied as is, unpeeled and in their skins.
2. Braai the pineapple slices and bananas over medium coals. The bananas are ready when they are completely black all over, and the pineapple is ready when the sugar on both sides has caramelised.
3. Remove from the fire and slice deep into the bananas along the inside curve. Open up the bananas by pressing simultaneously on both ends. Each banana should now look like an Indian canoe (paddle boat).
4. Put one banana and pineapple slice in each dessert bowl and place a scoop of ice cream into each banana. Cream or crème fraîche also works. Drizzle golden syrup or honey over the contents of each bowl and serve immediately.

BENCHMARK MALVA PUDDING IN A POTJIE

Some time in the late 1970s food guru Michael Olivier, who was responsible for the Boschendal Restaurant, asked his friend Maggie Pepler to come and teach them how to make the original malva pudding. Ever since, it's been a permanent fixture on their buffet menu. My malva pudding recipe is based on that original recipe and is published with Michael's blessing. The single biggest adjustment from the original recipe is that I bake the pudding in a no. 10 flat-bottomed baking potjie on the fire, and not in a conventional oven.

WHAT YOU NEED
(feeds 6)

FOR THE BATTER
1 cup flour
½ tot bicarbonate of soda
1 cup white sugar
1 egg
1 tot apricot jam
1 tot vinegar
1 tot melted butter
1 cup milk

FOR THE SAUCE
½ cup cream
½ cup milk
1 cup sugar
½ cup hot water
½ cup butter

WHAT TO DO

1. Light the fire. You'll need a steady supply of coals once the pudding is baking. Now use butter to grease your no. 10 flat-bottomed baking potjie.
2. Sift the flour and the bicarbonate of soda into a large bowl and stir in the sugar (you don't need to sift the sugar).
3. In another mixing bowl, whisk the egg very well. Now add the jam, vinegar, butter and milk, whisking well after adding each ingredient.
4. Add the wet ingredients of step 3 to the dry ingredients of step 2 and mix well.
5. Pour the batter into the potjie, put on the lid and bake for 50 minutes by placing some coals underneath the potjie and some coals on top of the lid. Don't add too much heat, as burning is a big danger. There is no particular risk in having too little heat and taking up to 1 hour to get the baking done, so rather go too slow than too fast. During this time, you can add a few fresh hot coals to the bottom and top of the potjie whenever you feel the pudding is losing steam.
6. When the pudding has been baking for about 40 minutes (about 10 minutes before it's done), heat all the sauce ingredients in a small potjie over medium coals. Keep stirring to ensure that the butter is melted and the sugar is completely dissolved, but don't let it boil. If you want a (slightly) less sweet pudding, use half a cup of sugar and a full cup of hot water for the sauce, instead of the other way around as per the ingredients list.
7. After about 50 minutes of baking, insert a skewer into the middle of the pudding to test whether it's done. If the skewer comes out clean, it's ready.
8. Take the pudding off the fire and pour the sauce evenly over it. Believe me, it will absorb all the sauce – you just need to leave it standing for a few minutes. Serve the malva pudding warm with a scoop of vanilla ice cream, a dollop of fresh cream or a puddle of vanilla custard. A good way to keep it hot is to put it near the fire, but not too close – after doing everything right, we don't want it to burn now.

AND ...

In the original recipe, the tot measures of apricot jam, butter and vinegar as well as the half tot of bicarbonate of soda are all given as 1 tablespoon each. These minor changes won't affect the outcome of the dessert but for the sake of accurately recording history, I think it's important that we note it.

FLAMBÉED PEACHES

This dish looks impressive yet preparing it is incredibly easy.

WHAT YOU NEED
(feeds 3–4)

1 x 420 g tin peach slices
a couple of tots brandy
vanilla ice cream (or cream
or custard)

WHAT TO DO

1. Open the tin and pour the peaches and syrup into a fireproof pan.
2. Position the pan over flames or coals. Stand the pan evenly so its ingredients don't spill.
3. Bring to the boil and let it simmer until the sauce starts to thicken. Now pour a generous dash of brandy into the pan and tip the pan towards the flames, setting the contents alight.
4. As soon as the flames have died down, the dessert is ready to serve with ice cream, cream or custard.

AND ...

If you are making this recipe for many people and use more than one tin of peaches, don't add the sauce from all the tins to the pan. The sauce gets a bit too much and will take a very long time to reduce and thicken.

When served with long-life custard or evaporated milk, this is a perfect recipe for a camping trip in the bush or on a deserted beach.

WORLD CUP WINNING BREAD PUDDING

There are two reasons why you should make the recipes in this book, and both these reasons are 100% applicable to what we have here: It's very easy and it tastes great. Your weapon of choice is a no. 10 flat-bottomed baking potjie. Everything that can possibly go wrong when making bread pudding is taken care of by the preparation method in this recipe. It is foolproof, it is the best bread pudding recipe in existence, and I hope you enjoy it as much as I do. If there were a World Cup of Bread Puddings, this one would not be knocked out in the semi-finals. It would win the trophy.

WHAT YOU NEED
(feeds 8)

½ cup raisins

½ cup dark rum

½ block butter (250 g)

1 cup brown sugar

1 tsp cinnamon powder

12 slices normal white bread

4 eggs

1 tin coconut milk (400 ml)

1 tot vanilla extract

ice cream or cream (optional, to serve)

WHAT TO DO

1. Marinate the raisins in the rum for at least an hour before you start work on this recipe, but a day of marinating is also fine.
2. Leave the butter outside your fridge for a few hours to soften as this will make the next step immensely easier.
3. Mix the soft butter, sugar and cinnamon together in a bowl and liberally spread this mixture on one side of all the slices of bread. Make sure you butter each slice right to its edges. Ration yourself so that there is enough cinnamon butter for all the slices but make sure that by the end you have used it all up.
4. Now cut the slices diagonally into halves, giving you 24 triangles. If you cut each one separately you need to slice 12 times but naturally you can stack them and slice a few at a time.
5. Arrange all of the bread triangles in the pot. There is no right or wrong way to do this; simply pack them into the potjie in whatever way you please.
6. Now scatter the rum-marinated raisins over the slices of bread in the potjie.
7. There is no reason to discard the raisin-infused rum. Pour it on ice with something like ginger beer and enjoy as a cocktail.
8. Whisk the eggs. A fork is fine, you don't need an actual whisk – this is not a cooking school exam.
9. Now mix the coconut milk and the vanilla essence with the whisked eggs. Pour this mixture over the bread and his friends in the pot. Put the lid on the pot and let the wet stuff soak into the dry stuff for a few minutes before baking.
10. With the lid still closed, bake for 30 minutes until firm and golden brown. This is a very easy process where you just need some coals underneath the pot and on top of the lid. Our aim here is that the sugar melts, the egg cooks and that the whole dessert is piping hot throughout. By the time all of this is done, the top exposed parts of the bread will be nice and crispy. These well-buttered but now crispy parts of bread add texture to the final product. As we buttered all slices of bread properly at the outset, they will not be dry, just crisp. It's one of the reasons why this is the best bread pudding ever.
11. You can serve it as is or with ice cream or whipped cream.

STICKY DATE AND PECAN NUT POTJIE

Not all desserts are created equal. This one is what we might call from a privileged background. It features both dates and pecan nuts which immediately give it the edge. To seal the deal it's also topped with a toffee sauce. It's the type of dessert that will feature on the menus of fancy restaurants, and that I will order when it's on those menus. Until the day comes in your life when you realise you can actually make an even better version of it in a potjie on the fire. There is not a single difficult task in this recipe. Just get the list of ingredients together and follow the steps. If you can read this book, you can make this dessert. The most difficult part will be finding the dates. They are hidden in the baking section of a supermarket. There will be a packet of pitted date pieces, compressed into a block, and that is what you're looking for. If you can't find it, ask anyone in the supermarket for directions. While you're in the baking section, also get some bicarbonate of soda and baking powder. From there make your way to the spice section and get some ginger powder in a little glass bottle. Everything else should be easy to find.

WHAT YOU NEED
(feeds 10)

FOR THE BATTER
250 g dates (chopped into small pieces)

1 tsp bicarbonate of soda

1 cup boiling water

½ cup butter (melted)

½ cup brown sugar (any shade of brown)

2 eggs

1 cup flour

1 tsp baking powder

1 tsp ginger powder

1 packet pecan nuts (100 g, roughly chopped)

FOR THE TOFFEE SAUCE
½ cup butter

1 cup light brown sugar

1 cup cream

1 tsp vanilla essence

WHAT TO DO

1. Throw the chopped dates and bicarbonate of soda into your no. 10 flat-bottomed baking potjie. Pour the boiling water over it and leave to stand for 10 minutes. The bicarbonate of soda is needed to break up the dates and make them softer and juicier, so you will see the texture and colour of the mixture changing during these 10 minutes.

2. Get a few coals under the potjie and add the butter and sugar to the dates in your potjie. Mix everything together and simmer on low heat until all the sugar is dissolved. We're not trying to cook anything, just getting the sugar to melt. Remove from the heat and let it cool down.

3. Once the mixture has cooled down (this will take about 10 minutes), add the eggs and mix well. Then add all of the other ingredients for the batter and stir well to combine them. Don't add the stuff for the sauce, just for the batter.

4. Put the lid on the potjie and bake on medium heat for about 30 minutes by placing coals underneath the potjie and on top of the lid. It's ready when you stick a knife into the pudding and the knife comes out without any raw dough sticking to the blade.

5. When you think the baking process is nearing the end, mix all the sauce ingredients together in a small pot or pan and bring to the boil. Simmer for 15 minutes until it starts to thicken, looks smooth and goes a rich brown toffee colour.

6. When the dessert in the potjie is ready, pour all the sauce over it so that it can soak in. Alternatively, dish up spoonfuls of the cakey dessert and pour sauce over each portion.

7. Serve with the type of trusted accompaniments you feel good about. These might include the likes of cream, ice cream and custard.

CARAMELISED NECTARINES WITH SPICED YOGHURT

The name says it all. Remember, the direct heat of the coals lets the sugar in the fruit caramelise, making it even sweeter. Enjoy!

WHAT YOU NEED
(feeds about 4)

6 nectarines
2 tots brown sugar

FOR THE SPICED YOGHURT
½ tsp ground cinnamon
3 cardamom pods
1 cup double-cream yoghurt

WHAT TO DO

1. Ground cinnamon is easy – just buy it.
2. With the cardamom you deal as follows. Break the pods open and use a pestle and mortar to grind the seeds into a fine powder. Failing a pestle and mortar, just put the seeds on a cutting board and roll over them with a wine bottle and some pressure until they are fine.
3. Mix the spices with the yoghurt.
4. Peel and halve the nectarines and remove the stones.
5. Braai the nectarines on a grid over hot coals until browned and then remove from the fire.
6. Sprinkle with sugar and return to the fire. Continue to braai them, turning each one to braai on both sides until the sugar melts and starts to bubble.
7. Serve the braaied nectarines with the spiced yoghurt.

AND ...

You can also use peaches for this recipe – whatever is in season at the time of braaing.

NUTELLA AND BANANA WRAPS

I don't think anyone needs an introduction to Nutella but if you do, welcome to earth and I hope you enjoy your stay. This dessert is very easy to make and very difficult to mess up. There is absolutely no preparation work to be done ahead of time. Hence, it's a good trick to have up your sleeve when you see the craving for dessert speaking to your guests at the end of a good braaied meal.

WHAT YOU NEED
(feeds 6–8)

1 jar Nutella (or similar chocolate hazelnut spread)

6 white flour wraps (buy them at a supermarket)

1 tot butter

6 bananas (peeled)

vanilla ice cream or whipped cream (to serve)

WHAT TO DO

1. Spread a layer of chocolate hazelnut spread on each wrap, making sure to spread all the way to the edges. The spread doesn't just add flavour to the dish; it will also serve as the glue and keep the wrap together. You probably won't have to finish the whole jar, but be generous.

2. Place your fireproof pan on the fire and add the butter. Cut the bananas in half, lengthwise, and fry for 3–5 minutes in the butter.

3. Place 2 fried banana halves on top of each other on the edge of the chocolate spread-covered side of a wrap and roll once. Now, at the ends of the bananas, tuck and fold the sides of the wrap to the inside so that the whole wrap is the length of the banana. Keep on rolling the banana tightly until you end up with something resembling a giant spring roll. Both ends will be closed, and the roll will be neat and tightly rolled. Prepare all 6 wraps this way.

4. Place the wraps on your grid and braai the wraps over medium heat. Use tongs to flip the wraps so that you braai them on all 4 sides. In total the braai should take about 8 minutes, depending on the heat of your coals, but please use your common sense as coals are not always the same after you've already had your main meal and returned to the braai area.

5. The wrap will be ready once the outside is crispy and toasted, and the banana on the inside is soft. Slice into halves and serve with ice cream or whipped cream.

SAGO PUDDING

Sago pudding is like my brother and sisters; something that I grew up with and that both my mother and my father love. The starchy white sago grains are made from a paste that comes from the sago palm, which grows in tropical places like the East Indies. But never fear – sago pudding is an authentic South African ending to a proper South African braai. In my family, we served sago with a sprinkling of cinnamon sugar and a bit of apricot jam, which you might or might not consider normal.

WHAT YOU NEED
(feeds 4–6)

1 litre milk (conveniently, almost every supermarket in the world sells milk in this measurement unit)

1 cup sago

½ cup sugar

2 tots butter

1 cinnamon stick

3 eggs

1 tsp vanilla essence

4 tots apricot jam

cinnamon sugar (see below)

WHAT TO DO

1. Throw the milk and sago into your flat-bottomed potjie and mix. Cover with the lid and let it stand for at least 1 hour – longer is also absolutely fine.
2. After an hour (or longer) add the sugar, butter and cinnamon stick to the sago and milk, then mix everything together. The butter will obviously not mix into the cold ingredients at this stage.
3. Put the potjie on the fire (coals or flames) and bring to a gentle simmer without the lid on. Control the heat (you might need to remove some coals or flames from under the potjie) and simmer gently for about 15 minutes until the grains have swollen up and the sago has become almost see-through. Don't multitask at this stage, as milk can easily boil over – you have been warned. If you're going to err on one side or another, rather simmer it for too long than too short, but please don't let it boil over or burn. Take the potjie off the fire and leave it to cool slightly with or without the lid on for at least 10 minutes (again, longer is acceptable).
4. Whisk the eggs and vanilla until they are well mixed and quite fluffy. Pour the mixture into the sago, stirring all the time.
5. Spoon the apricot jam in blobs on top of the sago mixture in the potjie, and then sprinkle with cinnamon sugar.
6. Put the lid on the potjie and bake for 30 minutes by placing coals underneath the potjie and also placing coals on its lid.

AND ...

To make the cinnamon sugar, just mix 1 teaspoon of ground cinnamon with 2 tots of sugar and stir well.

PEACHES IN PORT

The fact of the matter is, 'Peaches in Cape Vintage' does not have the same alliteration and ring as 'Peaches in port'. At the time of writing, port made in South Africa is called Cape Vintage though, and that is the wine I suggest you use for this recipe. The flavour profile is similar to Glühwein, and the port adds a fantastic sweetness while the peaches just soak up all the flavours. Be sure to reduce the sauce a bit as there is absolutely no damage done by letting the peaches cool down while the sauce reduces. This recipe is foolproof – just follow the steps and bask in the glory.

WHAT YOU NEED
(feeds 8)

8 peaches (fresh, peeled, but whole with the pip in)

8 black peppercorns

2 cinnamon sticks

2 star anise

2 cloves

2 cardamom pods

½ cup brown sugar

1 bottle port
(Cape Vintage wine)

ice cream (to serve)

WHAT TO DO

1. Peel the peaches. I find it works best with a vegetable peeler, and I find it works best to buy a new vegetable peeler if the one you currently have frustrates you.
2. Add all the ingredients, except the peaches and ice cream, to the potjie. Heat and stir until all the sugar is dissolved.
3. Put the whole peeled peaches into the potjie, cover with the lid, and cook for 30 minutes until the peaches are soft and sweet. If the peaches are not completely covered by port you can use your clean braai tongs to flip them over after 15 of the 30 minutes.
4. Remove the peaches and plate in dessert bowls.
5. Leaving the lid off, generate some more heat under the potjie and reduce the sauce a bit until you have just enough to divide among the 8 dessert bowls.
6. Serve the peaches with ice cream and pour the sauce reduction over that.

CHOCOLATE RISOTTO

This is a casual recipe – as in, you sit there and watch in awe whilst I casually whip up a chocolate risotto in a potjie on my fire. Add all the ingredients, make the chocolate sauce, add the rice and let it simmer until the rice is cooked. Try and stand in the shade and away from the brunt of your fire so as to not even break a sweat. It's part of the show.

WHAT YOU NEED
(feeds 6)

2 tots butter
2 tots cocoa powder
½ cup (125 ml) brown sugar
½ cup (125 ml) desiccated coconut
2 cups cream
1 tin coconut milk
1 cup milk
1 cup risotto rice

FOR SERVING
½ cup desiccated coconut
1 slab white chocolate
any type of cookies, biscuits or wafer chocolates (for example, Nuttikrust, KitKat or wafer biscuits)

WHAT TO DO

1. Place the potjie on the fire and get some fire under it. Toss the butter, cocoa powder, brown sugar and coconut in your pot. Stir-fry for 1 minute and immediately proceed to the next step.
2. Now add the cream, coconut milk, milk and risotto rice. Cook risotto over very mild to medium heat. You do not have to stir all the time, but with ingredients like milk and cream, you need to stir more often than not.
3. Let this slowly cook and simmer with the lid on the potjie, lifting the lid often to stir. Total cooking time is around 45 minutes so we're going slower here than with a more traditional savoury risotto as the cream and milk would appreciate a more gentle pace and be more inclined to stay in the potjie. The risotto rice will become thick and creamy once cooked and ready. If you think you need a bit more liquid to get the rice to that finish line, add a bit of water.
4. While the risotto is still cooking, roast your additional coconut in a pan for a few minutes until golden brown. If you don't have a pan, put the lid of the potjie on flames upside down.
5. Now, distribute the chopped or broken pieces of chocolate over the risotto, the same way you would do with Parmesan cheese if this was a savoury recipe. We do this so that you have streaks of white chocolate in the served meal. And we want that because it looks great. Also sprinkle the toasted coconut into the potjie.
6. Serve the risotto in bowls or cups, with a cookie, biscuit or wafer of your choice.

APPLE TART IN A POTJIE

I first learnt to make apple tart with my friend Louis Jonker, the renowned part-time chef from Stellenbosch (at home, he and his wife Anita split the cooking half-and-half). Once, during a visit to Ceres in the Western Cape, I decided to try something I'd never seen before (but it has since grown to such fame that it's now standard practice) – apple tart in a potjie! I adjusted the recipe slightly for cooking on a fire, and the end result was very successful. Try it and see for yourself!

WHAT YOU NEED
(feeds 6–8)

FOR THE FILLING
8–10 Granny Smith apples
(Louis and all the Ceres locals assured me that when baking apple tart, Granny Smith apples are the way to go)

½ cup water

½ cup raisins

1 tsp cinnamon

2 tots brandy (or rum)

FOR THE CRUMBLE
1½ cups cake flour

1½ cups brown sugar
(caramel brown sugar, or ordinary light brown sugar)

125 g salted butter
(a quarter of a 500 g block – soft)

another 2 tots butter

another dash of cinnamon

vanilla ice cream
(or cream, to serve)

WHAT TO DO

1. Peel and core the apples, cut them into chunks and throw them in a potjie. Add the water, raisins, cinnamon and brandy, and mix well.
2. Put the potjie on the fire, with the lid on. Cook the mixture for about 10 minutes until the apples begin to soften. Remove from the fire once cooked.
3. While the apples and their friends cook, add the flour, sugar and butter to a bowl and rub together with your clean fingertips until it forms a dry, crumbly mixture.
4. Add half of the crumble mixture to the potjie and mix it into the cooked apples.
5. Use the rest of the crumble mixture to cover the apples – make sure it spreads out evenly.
6. Add a couple of knobs of butter on top of the crumble and sprinkle a bit of cinnamon over the top to give the tart some colour. Put the lid on the potjie and go back to the fire.
7. Put the potjie over gentle coals and also put coals on the lid. When and if the coals lose power, add extra coals to the bottom and top of the potjie. If the fire is big and one side of the potjie gets more heat than the other, rotate the potjie every now and again. Bake for about 45 minutes to an hour, until you see the apple sauce bubbling through the crust when you lift the lid.
8. Enjoy with some vanilla ice cream or cream.

ISBN: 978-1-928257-67-7

First published by Bookstorm in 2019

Published by Bookstorm (Pty) Ltd
PO Box 4532
Northcliff 2115
Johannesburg
South Africa
www.bookstorm.co.za

Edited by Kelly Norwood-Young
Proofread by Salome Posthumus
Food styling by Christien Durand, Brita du Plessis
Photography by Guillaume Bosch, Matthys van Lill,
Minette Cilliers, Craig Kolesky, Sarah Isaacs
Cover and interior design by mr design
Printed by CTP Printers, Cape Town

INDEX